BOUNCING BACK

BOUNCING BACK

ATHLETIC TRANSITION SUCCESSES, FAILURES, AND LESSONS LEARNED ALONG THE WAY

PATRICK W. FINNEGAN

NEW DEGREE PRESS
COPYRIGHT © 2020 PATRICK W. FINNEGAN
All rights reserved.

BOUNCING BACK
Athletic Transition Successes, Failures, and Lessons Learned Along the Way

ISBN	978-1-63676-617-1	*Paperback*
	978-1-63676-290-6	*Kindle Ebook*
	978-1-63676-291-3	*Ebook*

> "Don't let the sum total of your existence
> be eight to ten pounds of air."
>
> —COACH JOHN THOMPSON JR.,
> GEORGETOWN UNIVERSITY

CONTENTS

	INTRODUCTION	11
CHAPTER 1.	WHAT AM I DOING HERE?	17
CHAPTER 2.	THE ATHLETE'S MINDSET	25
CHAPTER 3.	WHY IT MATTERS	39
CHAPTER 4.	A NEW VANTAGE POINT	53
CHAPTER 5.	TALK ABOUT IT	65
CHAPTER 6.	WHY YOU REALLY PLAYED	79
CHAPTER 7.	FIND A NEW TEAM	89
CHAPTER 8.	GEAR UP LIKE GAME DAY	99
CHAPTER 9.	GET BORED	109
CHAPTER 10.	THE ATHLETE'S DISTINCTION	121
CHAPTER 11.	ATHLETES' THOUGHTS, UNFILTERED	131
	ACKNOWLEDGMENTS	147
	APPENDIX	153

To my family—Mom, Dad, Cait, Ange, Grandpa Jim, Molly, Violet, and Hazel—please receive this as my formal submission for superior child, grandchild, sibling, and pet caretaker. Love you all. Your support enabled my improbable athletic journey and every success I've ever encountered and propelled me forward after every failure.

To my friends and loved ones and other supporters, thanks for always supporting me in good times and in not-so-good times.

To all of the generous people I spoke to for this book— thank you for your time, your wisdom, your candor, and your sincerity. This book stands on your shoulders.

Finally, to Grandpa Dan, Grandma Rie, and Grandma Jane—each of you influenced me in ways that I'm forever grateful for. May this book be a way for your impact on my life to be documented eternally.

INTRODUCTION

The book you're about to read is not really about me. Well, it kind of is. But it's also not. It's a book that's bigger than just my story.

This book is about the shared experiences between myself and other athletes leaving their sport behind. So to be clear, this book isn't supposed to be a preachy, self-help guide to athletic retirement success—I can assure you, there's one less twenty-six-year-old who thinks he has figured out life and all of its intricacies and nuance and is now prepared to share his "wisdom" with the masses. It's a book that's trying to consolidate the stories of athletes, myself included, and provide common perspectives and insights that may help other athletes.

It's really a book about better understanding the transition experience all competitive athletes must go through upon retirement.

When I set out to write this book, it began as a semi-cathartic activity for me, as a former athlete who had struggled with leaving my athletic identity behind, but as I researched and spoke to friends, teammates, and strangers, I realized I was far from the only one who had struggled with this experience. In fact, as I began to look into it more, nearly 90 percent of the former athletes I spoke to or interviewed experienced some form of emotional or mental distress in their retirement and transition phase.

So I set out to write this book, hoping to provide consolidated and concise insight on three subjects—a discussion and illumination of the issues athletes deal with upon retirement (I'll interchangeably use the term "transition" to describe this retirement experience as well), real-life stories about dozens of athletes and their own experiences, and a smattering of my own opinions and lessons learned from the conversations I had with those athletes in addition to my own experiences and ways to apply those lessons for athletes who may soon find themselves in the same boat as the rest of us.

So with that in mind, let's do a quick "SparkNotes" on me and why (I think) my words should matter to you at all. My name is Patrick Finnegan, and I was born and raised in Los Angeles, California, where I spent the first eighteen years of my life before moving to Washington, DC, to continue my football and educational pursuits at Georgetown University. My football career began at the ripe age of six for the Palos Verdes Pop Warner Mighty Mite 49ers and continued until age twenty-two. After providing four years of my football services and heart and soul for the Hoyas before the NFL decided not to come calling.

After a decade and a half of committing myself to football and reaping all of the life lessons and opportunities it provided for me, my retirement had come, and with it all of the challenges detailed above. I spent the better part of the next year and a half after athletics and graduation trying new activities and hobbies to fill the competitive void that was left when football and I parted ways: boxing, weightlifting, pick-up basketball, golf, competitive drinking (okay, not really, but senior spring of college sure felt like it was a competitive drinking tournament), and everything in between.

While each of these had its merits and in some ways managed to partially fill the void left by football, I still felt pretty unfulfilled, like a part of me I had cultivated over sixteen years of dedication was gone without a trace. As more time passed and I began to transition into my new life as an "adult," no longer playing a sport, I assumed maybe this phase would pass and everyone just finds that same competitive edge in their next major endeavor, such as their job. In my naivete, I decided this must be the case, and I'd find fulfillment in my chosen place of work.

For the first six to seven months of gainful employment, I worked and waited for the buzz I felt in athletics my whole life to return, expecting my job to snap its nonexistent fingers and whisk me away, back on the gridiron. But it didn't. In fact, despite that I enjoyed my job and learning a little bit about how to behave and how to find success in corporate America, I had yet to find the buzz I was searching for. It was a disheartening and a difficult time for me—a period of time where I openly wondered if the athlete I had identified as for my whole life to that point was going to need to be compartmentalized and forgotten, just someone who I used to be, but no longer really engaged. All of those melancholy thoughts swirled through my brain.

I learned during my researching process for this book this period was a common transition experience, a period of identity loss, driven by insufficient self-reflection. In short, I had never come to grips with what I was really giving up when football had ended. I had never identified what inherently existed within football that I loved, and I didn't have the structure or goal-setting mechanism that had defined my life from ages six to twenty-two to provide identity guardrails for my transition. I was dealing with mental and emotional anguish over losing the identity that had defined me for so long: I was an athlete for the entirety of my life, and then I was not.

That is, until I found my own way to "Bounce Back." With a little luck and a push from my brother to sign up for a marathon, I discovered a love of endurance running, a sport that requires physical dedication, structured training, mental toughness, and a certain "grit" factor. These were all aspects of athletics I had always found in football but had been missing in life after the fact. I had discovered an outlet for what I had inherently always loved about football, and I finally began to feel like an athlete again.

As my days began to get easier, with a new passion to pursue and a piece of my identity restored, I began to do some cursory research on athletic transitions and tried to educate myself on what resources were available for athletes who struggled with transitions the way I did. I assumed there had to be a better way forward than my path, because let's face it: not everyone will enjoy running the way I do.

What I found was a dearth of actionable advice.

The reality is there's really no clear or coherent answer readily available, despite Google providing a seemingly endless number of search results for "Athlete Transitions." So I found myself largely without an answer. As fate would have it, an opportunity to publish a book, working with a former McDonough School of Business professor at Georgetown, Eric Koester, stumbled within my purview by way of a LinkedIn connection and subsequent conversation. In what felt like an instant, I had found an opportunity to potentially impact the very issues I faced.

So the question I pose now is, why read this? Why me? Why you? Who are you?

Well, the short answer is read this because I think there's a chapter of the typical athlete's story that often goes untold. There exists plenty of documentation and stories about the paths to success in sport of every athlete, but far fewer about what happens when the game has concluded and the sport and the athlete go their separate ways. The post-retirement and end-of-career journey for me was and is a challenging one. It's a living process that requires thoughtful introspection, trial and error, and a great deal of effort to find a way to keep the identity of an athlete that was cultivated over years and years of hard work without playing the sport that created it. Our culture romanticizes athletes for their athletic success but often forgets or ignores the price that can come with the tireless dedication to athletic success.

Why you? Who are you? This one's a bit tougher: you might be an athlete on the precipice of retirement yourself. You might have retired six minutes ago, six months ago, twelve months ago, or twelve years ago. You might be the loved one of an athlete. You might have never been an athlete. You might not know what sports are! The answer's all the same: this book will give insight on what makes an athlete tick and why that very same mentality can cause problems in their transitions. It will do so through the stories of other athletes written from the perspective of one. If any part of that interests you, well you're in luck!

In telling the stories of the wide variety of former collegiate and professional athletes I had the pleasure of interviewing and researching, my hope is not to preach or provide an assertive list of must-do items to find competitive outlets for retired former athletes. I think that ship sailed after determining my wide range of athletes wouldn't agree on explicit pieces of transitional advice. It simply validated there certainly is no secret to success when it comes to transitioning to life after sports.

It's a challenging part of every athlete's life that all athletes must come to terms with. But there does seem to be a route to finding fulfillment without leaving behind the athlete that was once there. So while the athlete you may have known as a football player, a tennis star, a soccer wizard, a softball stud, may have retired from the sport you identified yourself with for the majority of your life, you can still find that persona in other places if you are willing to approach the next phase with the same sophistication and effort that was put in arriving at the top of your last one.

CHAPTER 1

WHAT AM I DOING HERE?

"What can I say... Mamba Out."

On April 13, 2016, standing at center court in a sold-out Staples Center in the heart of downtown Los Angeles, Kobe Bryant, fresh off willing his thirty-eight-year-old body to an inconceivable sixty-point outburst in his final NBA game, addressed tens of thousands of adoring fans in the arena and millions more watching on their televisions across the globe. In a two-minute, thirty-six-second love letter to those who cheered him and booed him through the highest of highs and lowest of lows in his twenty-year career with the Los Angeles Lakers, Kobe professed his gratitude to those who supported his journey.

From the day he entered the league as a fresh-faced, high-flying eighteen-year-old straight from high school until the end of his dominant, accolade-rich career as a five-time NBA Champion, Olympic Gold Medalist, Most Valuable Player, and one of the greatest competitors in the NBA's nearly century-old history. Kobe captivated audiences with his superlative play and with his ferocity and relentless drive to succeed, even earning the moniker "The Black Mamba" because of his "killer instinct" on the court. But on this night, as he said his farewell to his fans and to basketball, Kobe captivated the audience not only because of his outstanding play on the court, but because of the manner in which he spoke to the crowd after the game—sincerely, gratefully, and vulnerably.

> "It is not about the championships, it is about the down years," he explained to the thousands of fans in the arena and millions more watching on television across the globe, each hanging on his every word. "We did it the right way, we got our championships, and all I can do is thank you guys, thank you guys for all the support, thank you guys for the motivation, thank you guys for the inspiration."
>
> "This has been, this has been absolutely beautiful. I can't believe it has come to an end. You guys have been absolutely, absolutely beautiful. Thank you from the bottom of my heart. I love you guys, I love you guys."[1]

Kobe's final speech was an exclamation point on an athletic career successful enough to exceed that of the wildest imagination of young athletes around the globe, and he ended it as only Kobe could, with a dramatic two-word "buzzer beater" that left the world wanting more: "Mamba Out."

---

1   Deepak Vikraman, "Kobe Bryant last game: Read the entire transcript of Kobe's farewell speech," *International Business Times,* April 14, 2016.

But while Kobe had decided to leave the basketball world behind on that pivotal night, the question really on everyone's mind was, what's next? He can't really just walk away, can he? How does an athlete like Kobe, known for his unparalleled competitive drive and merciless demand for perfection, simply move on? What does someone like that do next?

But this question Kobe had to answer was not unique to Kobe.

Okay, in some ways it may have been unique to Kobe due to his vast abundance of fame and success, I'll grant that. Kobe was able to dictate the terms, and as we'll discuss in a bit more detail later, the circumstances of retirement matter. Kobe made the choice to retire: he wasn't pushed out of the game by Father Time or an inability to play; it was his choice. He also was granted a farewell tour of sorts: upon his retirement announcement, each city he played in showered him with applause, gifts, tokens of gratitude, and admiration for the entertainment he provided over the years. Kobe was "given his flowers" as he left the court, and he left the court on his own terms. So Kobe's retirement was in many ways very unique.

But in a bit more macro view, the question Kobe had to answer, "What's next?" is and was a question every athlete has to answer at some point in their life: for most, immediately at the conclusion of their athletic careers. This question slams the lion's share of new ex-athletes in the face similarly to how I'd imagine an unexpected right hook from Mike Tyson might feel—a period of shock and immense pain followed by a daze and disorientation that leaves you asking which direction is up. And this period of difficulty is driven not by a singular event, but rather by, up to that point, a lifetime of commitment to the pursuit of the peak of athletic success—a peak which is very finite.

There are a finite number of positions available in a finite number of sports at a finite number of levels. Each year, more than eight million US high school students, 480,000 NCAA student athletes, and roughly ten thousand professional athletes who compete on behalf of their respective teams.[2] For better perspective, those numbers reflect 2 percent, 0.1 percent, and 0.002 percent of the United States population, respectively. But hidden in those deceiving numbers are the amount of annual former athletes. Annually on the back end of these numbers are 1.8 million retired high school athletes, 115,000 retired collegiate athletes, and hundreds of retired professional athletes, some by their own volition and others who simply have reached the end of their athletic rope—whether they'd like to acknowledge it or not. According to a study done by the NCAA in 2015, of what I'll call the five major professional sports in America—football, baseball and softball, basketball, soccer, and hockey—over 40 percent of D-1 collegiate athletes in their respective sports anticipated continuing their sport professionally or in the Olympics after college.[3] See the problem?

---

2   Erin Irick, "NCAA Sports Sponsorship and Participation Rates Report," accessed March 6, 2020.

3   Lydia Bell et al., "Results from the 2015 GOALS Study of the Student-Athlete Experience," Report presented at the NCAA Convention, (San Antonio, Texas: Grand Hyatt San Antonio, 2016), 129, accessed May 4, 2020.

Now why did I just inundate you with enough numbers to wish you paid more attention during AP Statistics in high school? Because when a highly competitive athlete retires or is retired from his or her sport, if you will, they often lose more than just a hobby, an event, or something to pass the time. In many cases, when an athlete's days as an athlete are done, they lose a piece of their identity—a piece of themselves they've cultivated, in some cases, for the vast majority of their lives. Years of hard work and cliched bodily fluids (blood, sweat, tears, and the like) have been poured into the athlete's respective craft and have woven themselves into the fabric of the athlete's personality. In fact, and in most cases, upon retirement, the athlete has lost an outlet for their personality to shine.

If you were doing some sharp mental math in the paragraph above, you would have caught with all of the turnover at each level of athletics, you're looking at somewhere near two million athletes annually who become former athletes at the blow of the final whistle.

So as data points would have you understand it, if there are really that many people going through this struggle, shouldn't we have a simple solution? There has to be a one-size-fits-all approach that can help athletes feel less isolated, depressed, or uncertain when they leave sports, right? How else does this occur annually?

***

"Post-grad and life after sports humbled me very quickly, that's for sure."

"For the most part no one else was looking out for me. In professional life everyone has their own goals, and they don't often really align with your own."

Anthony Perasso and Casey Kuhns are two former Division 1 collegiate athletes whose names most of you may not recognize at first glance (I can say this comfortably because both also happen to be dear friends of mine, sorry gents). As you can tell from their respective quotations above, both Perasso, a four-year varsity oarsman at Boston College, and Kuhns, a four-year varsity linebacker and teammate of mine at Georgetown, are in the same category as former Division 1 athletes who had to navigate the difficult transition of life after athletics at the conclusion of their collegiate careers—even though neither truly had aspirations of advancing their athletic careers professionally. Both Kuhns and Perasso approached their transitions anticipating a level of fulfillment from their professional workplace, but found different things

Kuhns explained the loss of the locker room driven by a common goal was most difficult, saying, "Although a sales job has allowed me to be competitive and to be part of a 'team,' I quickly learned that for the most part no one else was looking out for me. In professional life, everyone has their own goals, and for the most part they don't align with your own. I missed the camaraderie created from being on a team where everyone shared the same goals."

Perasso, on the other hand, divulged that the identity shock that came with leaving behind sport created a larger hurdle for him. "So much of that self-esteem was previously derived from being an athlete, for better or for worse, so post-grad was humbling in that way for sure. Going from a senior on a college campus proudly wearing my team gear to class and having a team of people who really care about me and who I really care about and then letting that all go. Having a company tell you you're worth minimum wage. That will force you to find some meaning in your life identity outside of athletics, which isn't easy."

Both Perasso and Kuhns, as we'll discuss periodically throughout the rest of the book, have taken different approaches to transition and have different perspectives on what makes the transition out of sports difficult. What makes that distinction important, however, is on the surface and demographically speaking they are categorized the same way—former Division 1 athletes from high academic universities who dedicated four years of collegiate life to chasing an athletic dream and were forced to find new purpose and achievement outside of athletics upon graduation. Which is precisely the point—two different athletes taking two different paths and living two different transition experiences.

***

So if there are so many people dealing with this issue, but there's not a singular right answer... then what?

Well, the answer I've landed on, and the reason I've written this book, is this: no transition experience should or will be handled the same way, and there is no one-size-fits-all solution. But there are core underlying principles both Anthony, Casey, and the other athletes who I interviewed and researched, knowingly or unknowingly, provided that can at the very least help the next generation of athletes leaving their sport do so a bit more smoothly.

CHAPTER 2

THE ATHLETE'S MINDSET

To give appropriate credence to the idea that finding an answer to "what's next" is both important and possible for all former athletes, I believe we need to discuss the circumstantial factors and the environment that cultivates the athlete's mindset that makes the transition challenging in the first place.

It was not simply the action of retiring from football that was the genesis of my struggle trying to figure out what was next, but rather the fact I lost the outlet for my athletic identity and subsequently lost the sense of who I was. I had spent the vast majority of my life constantly competing for and chasing a dream of professional athletic glory, and suddenly that dream was gone. I found myself without a competitor and smack in the middle of an identity crisis.

But what caused that identity crisis? What drove me to feeling like a balloon I had spent sixteen years filling up had suddenly popped?

Well, it was exactly that.

My identity felt like it was stolen from me because of how long I had spent cultivating it. I spent time and effort and I sacrificed to make it to the level I did. The challenges I faced were driven by the fact I found myself without a playing field, a competitor, a measuring stick of my success, and thus was left identifying as an athlete without an athletic competition. However, to understand why these transitions are hard for former athletes, like it was for me, it's first important to understand the two main components I believe make an athlete's mindset and identity different.

When I interviewed former athletes for this book, while discussing the transition phase of retirement, each athlete I spoke to made a point, in some way, shape, or form, to distinguish the loss of competition was chief among their struggles. No matter what profession or hobby the former athlete ended up identifying as their method of moving forward, each referenced the need for competition in their lives. But why is that?

It seems quite logical athletes desire fierce competition: after all, competition is in the definition of sport, as defined by the Cambridge Dictionary: "a game, competition, or activity needing physical effort and skill that is played or done according to rules, for enjoyment and/or as a job."[4] Competition is athletics and athletics is competition. But why would the loss of competition be such a challenging transition for athletes to make? I'll posit that competition provides a measuring stick of sorts that allows deficiencies and areas of growth to be highlighted, and thus a structure by which

---

4   Cambridge Dictionary, s.v. "sport (n.)", accessed March 15, 2020.

an athlete can improve. Sports provide a very clear definition and playing field the athlete can compete on and be judged upon—an arena and a measuring stick that is less obviously available in other aspects of life.

***

One of my favorite stories of competition among elite athletes comes from none other than one Michael Jordan, a former superstar guard for the Chicago Bulls (and the Chicago White Sox of the MLB and the Washington Wizards, for that matter). A six-time NBA champion and widely accepted as the greatest basketball player to ever live (and to be abundantly clear, no, we will not be having this debate in this book). Jordan's competitive drive is well-documented and includes countless tales of his unparalleled work ethic and drive to be great. Jordan was relentless and ruthless and would do anything for an edge on or off the basketball court, consistently creating rivalries and chips on his shoulder only he knew were there.

So on an innocuous night in the middle of March 1993, when a relatively unknown and unheralded player named LaBradford Smith of the Washington Wizards lit up the floor with thirty-seven points, many of them scored while being defended by Jordan, Michael took notice. Smith was by no means the same caliber of player as Jordan, but on that particular night, he had Jordan's number, and according to Jordan, after the game, let Jordan know about it, saying mockingly, "Nice game, Mike."

So what did Jordan do? His competitive fire lit, playing again the next night against Smith and the Wizards, Jordan proceeded to score thirty-six points in the first half, supposedly in homage to Smith's stellar performance from the night before. Jordan finished with forty-seven points en route to a dominant Bulls victory. Jordan had exacted his revenge on Smith, letting him know despite Smith's nice game the night before, Jordan would undoubtedly one-up him. An example of Jordan's outrageous competitive drive and ruthlessness, right? Now consider, not only did Smith not mock Jordan after his scoring outburst during the first game, but he didn't say anything at all. Jordan made up the whole story in a ruse to light his own competitive fire and give him the edge he needed to punish Smith and the Wizards the next day.[5] Jordan was so competitive he was willing to quite literally create nonexistent enemies to push himself further.

Competition is a crucial part of the athletic mindset that is cultivated throughout an athlete's life. Competition is what provides the road map for the athlete to determine how they can improve and eventually reach the top of their respective sport. Athletes spend the majority of their careers focusing on how to get to the next level of competition and how to move past their current level, and competition provides a measuring stick of success and progress.

Marina Paul, a former Georgetown University women's soccer captain and All-Big East defender, who we'll meet in more

---

5   Sam Quinn, "Michael Jordan vs. LaBradford Smith: A look at the Bulls legend's revenge against an imaginary opponent," *CBS Sports,* May 17, 2020.

detail later, described the competitive mindset in a similar vein: "There's an intersect between being on a team and being hyper-competitive and always wanting to win [that you develop in sports]. It's translatable even, like when you have a deliverable, and there's someone who is a lead, someone is a sub lead, and then you have support, whoever else. And I think it's knowing that we are achieving 'X' goal together, and we're all on this team, because we all want to win. But at the same time, within this team, I'm so innately driven that I will be here until whatever time it takes to get this done, or like, we'll sit and go like word by word to make sure that this slide is perfect. Being able to have this camaraderie and this teamwork, but also being so driven and competitive that you want to do the best that you can, and having people support you in that."

However, when an athlete leaves their sport behind, their ability to gauge progress and success has been removed. In "Managing the transition into retirement from sport for elite athletes" from Sheffield Hallam University in Sheffield, England, the authors highlight that a fundamental issue with athletes transitioning comes from the loss of a sense of control of their environment because they no longer have the structure sport provides: "This lack of personal control may cause problems for athletes when adjusting to their non-sporting identity after retirement, due to the loss of structure, routine, and discipline to which they were previously accustomed. Many athletes report that being excluded from the social practices of their sport, as well as the loss of camaraderie with teammates and the joy of competition, were key parts of their sporting life which they struggled to replace after retirement."⁶ The loss of a competitive outlet creates a fundamental hole in the identity of an athlete and the way in which they view progress and success. This in turn begins to chip away at the identity of the athlete.

***

Where most would agree and inherently understand competition is central to an athlete's identity, fewer may understand that so too is sacrifice.

Have you ever considered what you would give up to find success? Have you thought about where you would draw the line in the sand to reach your goals? Is there even a line? Is there anything you wouldn't do? Would you be willing to expose your personal life to the broader public? Would you be willing to take on uncommon roles and responsibilities in your personal life, in your social life, and in your public life?

Each of these (non-exhaustive) rhetorical questions are thoughts regularly considered by anyone who is chasing down a goal, not simply athletes. However, in the case of elite athletes, the consequences of the answers to each of these questions is heightened. With every answer comes new risks, new rewards, and new ramifications.

Nestled along the Northeastern border of a landlocked country surrounded by seven neighbors in Central Europe is the

---

6   Chris Hattersley et al., "Managing the transition into retirement from sport for elite athletes," (Sheffield, UK: Sheffield Hallam University, 2019), accessed March 13, 2020.

capital city of Austria. It is home to 20 percent of the nine million people who reside in the East alpine country. From 1992 until 1994 it was home to an eight-year-old child from Fresno, California, nearly 6,500 miles across the globe, with dreams of soccer stardom. Michael Chabala, an NCAA Men's Soccer All-American, a two-time Major League Soccer (MLS) Cup Champion, and a ten-year veteran of the MLS, was sent to Austria at the ripe old age of eight to begin formal training for the dreams he would later realize. But Austria is not where Michael's journey began.

Fresno, California, sits in the San Joaquin Valley of Central California and is home to roughly five hundred thousand Californians, making it the fifth most populous city of California. Fresno is known primarily for its large-scale agricultural footprint, its relative equidistant location from the major California cities of San Francisco, Sacramento, and Los Angeles, and much less so for its ability to churn out prodigious athletes. However, like most kids who eventually become elite athletes, Michael proved to be an exception. Like most children, Mike's introduction to soccer began at a young age in his local area leagues, but he found he had an uncommon love of the game at an early age.

"My earliest memories, all I can remember was just being freakishly excited, you know, overly obsessed, and I just couldn't sleep the night before and I would lay everything out... My whole uniform would be laid out on the floor, literally shoes to shin guards and socks, literally everything," Chabala said. "I look back on it now and there was some type of fireball, some type of magic wand, or some spell that had hit me at that age and just provided clarity, even at that age, like, 'Okay, this is what you're going to do,' 'This is what your deal is,'" and as time would tell, he was right.

Chabala excelled through the earliest beginnings of his soccer career, proving even as early as seven he wasn't just another good young soccer player. Mike's play began drawing the attention of local club teams and coaches interested in bringing him onto their traveling teams' rosters, with coaches regularly requesting his parents to let him play for their teams.

There was one noticeable gap in Chabala's skill set that created a problem for all parties—his age. The club teams interested in Mike all had minimum age requirements to play on their teams, usually reserved for children aged eleven and up, but for all his talents on the field, Mike could not control the fact he was only seven years old at the time. So what did he and the other coaches do? Well, with a nod, wink, and a handshake, the seven-year-old child managed to find himself competing with kids nearing the precipice of puberty and a traveling club team to provide him with the next level of competition. But it was soon thereafter the opportunity that would change the trajectory of his soccer dream forever would arrive upon Mike's doorstep.

The San Diego Surf Cup is an amateur soccer tournament held annually in, who could've guessed, San Diego, California, and according to its website, "[is] the premier summer tournament for youth soccer, featuring the top teams in the nation and attracting more than 500 college and scouts. The Surf Cup is played at [one of] the best [facilities] in the nation, featuring up to 22 full-sized fields on pristine grass.

Every year, Surf Cup flies in the best referees in the region to match the level of the best teams in the nation who will come together to produce epic match ups."

Self-congratulating biases aside, the San Diego Surf Cup is objectively a big deal in the world of amateur soccer, and in the case of Mike, would be a big deal in laying the foundation for his soccer career. It was there, at the San Diego Surf Cup in 1992, Mike's performance would be noted by a scout from a first-division Austrian Bundesliga team, FK Austria Wein.

Following a conversation with Mike's coaches and Mike's parents, the scout and trainer from the team would spend the next weeks working with Mike independently and evaluating his performance and potential. Shortly thereafter, the offer was presented, and a turning point in the career of a young Michael Chabala had arrived: would he be willing to move to Austria to join FK Austria Wein's developmental program? To leave his family behind at eight years old? Perhaps more importantly, would his parents be willing to let him make that sacrifice?

"It was a perfect storm, right?" Chabala explained to me, "My dad was always pushed aside because of my grandpa's military career, so nothing was ever about his sports or nothing was ever really about the family or him. It was about my grandpa's career and traveling and moving. And then on my mom's side, she's one of four. So my grandparents were always split, sharing finances and making sure that they were always trying to equal out like the love to all of the kids so there wasn't ever an emphasis for them. And so I think when my mom and dad were becoming parents and thinking about how they wanted to raise my sister and I, they both were like, 'We want to give our kids the best opportunity to be able to do whatever they want to do.'" In the case of a burgeoning soccer career, Mike's best opportunity was to go abroad to Vienna, Austria, and train with FK Austria Wein's Youth Academy.

"I think that was like a really pivotal moment for me," he said about spending the better part of three years traveling back and forth from Fresno to Vienna for months at a time, living with an Austrian host family and training daily with the club. "It really accelerated my career."

This sacrifice Michael and his family made is extraordinary and represents much more of the exception than the norm. The idea to be uncommon and elite in the highest level of anything you must be willing to take uncommon risks and take on uncommon sacrifices is not new. Sayings like "No Risk, No Reward" or "You gotta risk it to get the biscuit" exist because this idea is easily understood (and catchy, for what it's worth). However, what makes these sacrifices and risks, such as sending away your eight-year-old child and deciding as an eight-year-old to go abroad to Austria to play professional soccer, common to athletics is often these seemingly Herculean sacrifices aren't viewed as sacrifices to the athlete at all. In fact, the athlete is so enamored with the chase of success the supposed sacrifices are an enjoyable part of the journey.

***

Take it from Brandi Chastain, former USWNT soccer star and 1999 World Cup hero, who said, "I honestly and humbly answer that I don't feel I sacrificed anything. I made the choices I did to play soccer and become a member of the US Women's National Team because I loved it," or from eleven (eleven!) time Olympic medalist Natalie Coughlin, who explained, "I can't think of any ONE thing that I've given up to reach my goals... it's been a lifetime of making choices that have ultimately affected my swimming career."[7]

There are countless examples of athletes eschewing the idea of sacrifice and redefining it instead as a "decision." Decisions around health, social interactions, time management, and more often seem like sacrifices to the average person are often brushed aside as necessary steps on the path to success for the athlete. Because of this, I believe a primary differentiation that distinguishes the mindset of an athlete is the ability to simplify complex decisions into binary ones boiled down to the simple question: does this get me closer to my goal? Will getting up early in the morning during the offseason to work out make me a better football player? Will focusing on eating right leading up to the week before a race allow me to PR during the swim meet? Will deciding not to go out and grab beers on a Thursday keep me fresh for my game on Sunday? Will leaving my family to go to a foreign country at eight years old allow me to chase my dream of being a professional soccer player? What would you give up to follow your dream? As admirable as these questions may seem, there is a price to this mindset and ability to eschew

---

7   Todd Kuslikis, "18 of the greatest athletes on earth share their insights on the sacrifices it takes to get to the top," A Shot of Adrenaline (Blog), May 2012.

sacrifice: the more you've spent sacrificing and climbing the ladder of athletics, the more difficult your transition can be.

Sacrifice in the name of the pursuit of a goal is ingrained in the mindset of an athlete. It is the thought process that unilaterally drives elite athletes to separate themselves from their peers and separates an athlete engaged in sport as a passion from one engaged as a hobby. However, this sacrifice helps cultivate a singular sense of identity between the person and their athletic identity. That can create issues during the transition from athletics to retirement. Again from "Managing the transition into retirement from sport for elite athletes," the authors present the idea the closer an athlete identifies themselves with their athletic identity, the more difficult their transition can be, primarily because of the challenges presented by "reorganizing one's personal and social goals once sport is no longer the main 'priority' in a person's life." [8]

In the conversations I've had with athletes and the research I've done, this has rung true across the board. The ability to handle the transition, and thus the "lull" of the transition, was more palatable for athletes who identified less with their athletics than those who had a more united view of themselves as an athlete first and foremost. But the foundation that causes the struggle with transitioning is oftentimes when an athlete has sacrificed so much in the name of athletic glory and pursuit there is a difficulty separating the identity and

---

8   Chris Hattersley et al., "Managing the transition into retirement from sport for elite athletes," (Sheffield, UK: Sheffield Hallam University,2019), accessed March 13, 2020.

successes as an athlete from their identity as a person, a concept similar to the idea of identity foreclosure.[9]

Identity foreclosure, in a brief summary as it relates to this book, rests on the following argument: personal identities are formed at young ages through varied experiences; an athlete, or anyone with a passion that consumes the vast majority of their time or experiences, has fewer varied experiences, and thus finds themselves more susceptible to attaching their identity prematurely to an occupation or ideology.[10] In many cases with athletes, because a majority of their ultimate successes at a young age in life have been at their chosen sport, there is a natural tendency to tie one's worth and identity to that sport. The more sacrifices an athlete has made in pursuit of their athletic goals, the more they will identify holistically as an athlete, and the more difficult it can be to transition into life without sport.

To best evaluate how to help athletes transition into life after their playing days are over, we first must understand what causes athletes to struggle when the transition occurs. There are many typical components that make up the athlete's mindset and this by no means is an exhaustive or mutually exclusive compilation of those factors. But I'd argue the loss of the athlete's identity is the chauffeur of challenges that drives a struggling period during the transition after

---

9   Evelyn Monteal Oregon, "An Examination of Athletic Identity and Identity Foreclosure Among Male Collegiate Student-Athletes," (Chapel Hill, NC: University of North Carolina at Chapel Hill, 2010), accessed June 13, 2020.

10 Ibid.

competitive sports. The engine of that car is competition and sacrifice.

CHAPTER 3

WHY IT MATTERS

Struggling after retirement is normal. Period. Full stop. It's normal. It's normal and it's okay.

I want to make sure if no other message is out there in this book, the above is understood. It's okay to be okay, too—maybe your transition hasn't been as hard as you may have anticipated. If so, that's great! But even more importantly, if you are struggling after retirement from sports, you should feel comfort in knowing you are absolutely, 100 percent, unequivocally not alone in your struggles.

In fact, in my research, interviews, and studies, an overwhelming majority of discussion on this topic is about how pervasive an issue, the struggling period, can be for former athletes. This chapter is most likely the one all of you readers (or perhaps just one reader; at the time of writing this, I may be the only buyer of my own book) were curious if I would discuss—the implications of the struggle and thus the mental health of the athlete after retirement. But first, let's level set on expectations here: I'm not an expert in mental health. I have no PhD, no masters, not even a psychology major nor minor. However, when I set out to do research on this topic, I discovered reliable data on the subject is quite scarce.

**

Many doctors, psychologists, and philosophers have set out to address the correlations between the retirement of the athlete and the challenges that have been faced after and have created compelling logical and defensible arguments. As we discussed in the previous chapter, there is well-documented evidence that athletes face an identity crisis upon retirement and identity crises can leave former athletes in difficult positions emotionally, financially, and socially, much like any other personal crisis. These problems are not isolated to one specific sport or one specific level. In fact, there are many examples of former superstars who have publicly struggled much in the same way that I, very much not a former superstar, struggled. It's also important to note not every athlete struggles in the same way, nor does the retirement phase affect all athletes in the same manner. In "Career Development and Transitions of Athletes," a global scholarly study examining the roles of contextual factors of athletic transition and retirement, the authors address there are in fact, noticeable differences in the transition phase of athletes depending on their sport, their gender, and their country.[11]

However, as succinctly stated in the preface of the scholarly article "Athlete identity and reactions to retirement from

---

11   Natalia B. Stambulova et al., "Career development and transitions of athletes: the International Society of Sport Psychology Position Stand Revisited," *International Journal of Sport and Exercise Psychology*, March 2020.

sports:" "The arguments connecting athletic identity to post-retirement adjustment difficulties are compelling. And yet, once again, few direct empirical demonstrations of this relationship can be found."[12] To the fault of no one, there is a fundamental issue in trying to collect strong statistics on this subject. Scholars and researchers alike have struggled to find a sufficient empirical link between the ideas, in my opinion, because it is still taboo subject matter to discuss, especially among athletes. The subject matter at hand requires honest internal feedback to be provided. Because of this, most of the academic studies done on the subject are done on retiring athletes and focused on asking former athletes about the circumstances of their retirement and the scaled "success" of their transition, in hopes of quantifying thoughts and feelings.

For example, the NCAA and Gallup in 2016 decided to do this by exploring the question, "How do former student-athletes and non-student athletes compare on various measures of well-being?" Their joint research paper, "Understanding Life Outcomes of Former NCAA Student-Athletes," explored the "outcomes" of a significant sample of collegiate graduates, both former student-athletes and non-student-athletes as named in the study, based on the Gallup-Purdue Index.[13] For those of you who are not immediately and intimately familiar with the Gallup-Purdue Index (Read: me), the "GPI"

---

12   William M. Webb et al., "Athlete Identity and Reactions to Retirement from Sports," *Journal of Sport Behavior* 21, no. 3 (09, 1998): 338-362.

13   Gallup Inc., "A STUDY OF NCAA STUDENT-ATHLETES: Undergraduate Experiences and Post-College Outcomes," 2020, accessed March 20, 2020.

is defined as "the first measure to evaluate the long-term success of graduates in their pursuit of great jobs and great lives, as measured by the Gallup Employee Engagement Index and Gallup-Sharecare Well-Being Index, respectively. The Gallup-Purdue Index examines college experiences such as internship participation, involvement in extracurricular activities, relationships with professors, and having student loans."[14] The Employee Engagement Index and the Well-Being Index are determined through a variety of surveys, questionnaires, and interviews of a randomized and statistically significant sample and "scored" based on their answers. The Well-Being Index focuses on five main categories or factors of well-being when determining its score: Purpose, Social, Financial, Community, and Physical, relating to motivation, relationships, financial security, community involvement, and health and wellness, respectively.

In layman's terms, the Gallup-Purdue Index attempts to evaluate college graduates' happiness based on their professional engagement and their general well-being. So there you have it, Aristotle, happiness equals professional engagement plus general well-being. Sure doesn't seem like you needed eleven books and ninety-five thousand words to get to that conclusion. Jokes aside, the NCAA and Gallup made an intellectual effort at trying to determine if former collegiate student-athletes tend to be more fulfilled than their non-student-athlete peers—and the results were intriguing.

When it came to employee engagement, or the first term in the "Happiness Equation," as I've decided to refer to it,

---

14 Ibid.

student-athletes were just as likely to be engaged at work as non-student-athletes, with 42 percent of student-athletes and 39 percent of non-student-athletes reporting "Engaged." [15]

The study found in the second term of our "Happiness Equation," on average, student-athletes are more likely to be "Thriving" in four of the five elements of the Well-Being Index, namely the Purpose, Social, Community, and Physical categories. In addition, student-athletes are as likely as non-student-athletes to be "Thriving" in the Financial category. Even more interestingly, in the "Purpose" category, defined as "Liking what you do each day and being motivated to achieve your goals," a majority (56 percent) of student-athletes identified as "Thriving."[16]

With all of this in mind, the NCAA and Gallup report's final conclusion was "Former student-athletes are significantly more likely to be 'thriving' in four out of five areas, ... [demonstrating] that former student-athletes are excelling in multiple areas of well-being."[17] Effectively, the conclusive point the report makes is the average former collegiate student-athlete generally seems to find their purpose after college better than the non-student-athlete.

***

A primary roadblock for running proper empirical surveys and studies on the subject matter is false information. No, I

---

15   Ibid.
16   Ibid.
17   Ibid.

am not accusing anyone of lying, but when I say false information, I mean to suggest there are a number of confounding variables when asking people to be introspective about their feelings.[18] The nature of studies like the above can prove challenging because of the inherent difficulty of quantifying nonquantitative thoughts and expressions that may be confounded by apprehension or an overly optimistic or pessimistic attitude of the subjects. With all of the above being said, I'd like to present the full picture of the mental health and transition impact both anecdotally and academically so you, the reader (or again, if it's still just me talking to myself), can hopefully empathize with the stories told and also feel educated on the current state of academic research on the subject. While the academic research continues, the most impactful way to continue the educational effort for you, the reader, in my opinion, is to educate anecdotally.

Chris Conte is a former National Football League (NFL) defensive back who I had the pleasure of interviewing about this exact topic. A Southern California kid, Conte was a standout two-way player (meaning he played both offense and defense) at Loyola High School (of which I also am a proud alum, Go Cubs) before embarking on a stellar three-year career at the University of California at Berkley. Chris made the leap roughly 1 percent of all aspiring football players make when he was drafted by the Chicago Bears in the third round of the 2011 NFL draft. After eight impressive

---

18 Norbert Schwarz, "Feelings as information: Informational and motivational functions of affective states," in *Handbook of Motivation and Cognition* edited by E.T. Higgins, R Sorrentino, Guilford Press, 1990, accessed May 13, 2020.

years in the NFL as a starting defensive back for both the Bears and the Tampa Bay Buccaneers, Chris retired in 2019 to move onto the next chapter of his life. For those who are less familiar with the NFL, the average NFL career is roughly three years—Chris nearly tripled that lifespan.

But despite his immense success, Conte pointed out reaching the pinnacle of his sport actually had some unintended consequences: "For guys like me, guys that did play in the NFL, it [can be] harder to find that next career because you've had no work experience, and all you have really going for you is you're an athlete that dedicated your life to playing sports. Which I think does mean something in the business world. But even for me, I left school early without finishing my degree because I was all-in on football." This was a common sentiment among professional athletes I spoke to and researched, as most made some point of acknowledging that while they were grateful for the doors their athletic abilities opened, there were other opportunities that passed them by.

Fellow NFL alum and New York Football Giants all-time leading rusher Tiki Barber said in an interview with ESPN's Jeffri Chadiha in 2012, "It's hard for an athlete because you take a different path when you leave college than other kids. For ten years, you're doing your thing while those other people are climbing the corporate ladder and growing up. Once you get into that game, your peers are much higher than you and you're thirty-something years old. You feel like you can't really catch up."[19]

---

19   Jeffri Chadiha, "Life after NFL a challenge for many," *ESPN.com*, May 31, 2012.

The late Roy Halladay, one of the greatest pitchers of the twenty-first century and a member of the professional baseball Hall of Fame, according to a friend interviewed for ESPN's 30 for 30 documentary, *Imperfect: The Roy Halladay Story*, made his thoughts quite clear on the difficulties of the transition when he asked, "Man, how the f--- do you do this?"[20] All of which is to say the transition from professional sports often leaves athletes feeling well out of their element for the first time in many of their lives.

What comes of this discord? "A period of depression for sure, where you're just trying to figure things out," Conte explained. "It takes time to really kind of get settled back and feel like you're doing things that are important again."

This concept is addressed by Thomas and Ermler in "Institutional obligations in the athletic retirement process," explaining oftentimes when an athlete has spent their career developing a particular set of skills, in this case their athletic ability, it can be quite traumatic when those skills are no longer transferable: "The skills the athlete has perfected for so long are now useless in a world that no longer sees him or her as special. Much of our personal identity and self-esteem rests on what we are able to do cognitively, affectively, and physically. To be able to do nothing very skillfully in the real world ... is to be cast into nothingness, loneliness, and isolation."[21]

---

20 *Imperfect: The Roy Halladay Story*, Directed by Mike Farrell and Brian Rivera, aired May 29, 2020, on ESPN.

21 Kathy L. Ermler et al., "Institutional Obligations in the Athletic Retirement Process," *Quest*, 40:2, 137-150. 1988.

In addition to questioning the impact or value they can have on a non-athletic field of play, some athletes tend to struggle with the loss of glamour and fame that accompanies elite athletic success. "I think the hardest thing, the hardest thing for a lot of guys, is the mental side of [retirement]. They struggle with the loss of fame and glory—the notoriety, the feeling like they're somebody, feeling like they're important. I think [many former players] struggle with going from a stadium that's filled with a bunch of people to realizing you're never going to be able to recreate that. So I think it causes a lot of depression for a lot of guys," Conte explained. Even former boxing great, 1976 Olympic Gold Medalist, and five-weight-class boxing champion of the world Sugar Ray Leonard once said, "Nothing could satisfy me outside the ring... There is nothing in life that can compare to becoming a world champion, having your hand raised in that moment of glory, with thousands, millions of people cheering you on."[22]

The common vein between both of these scenarios is in each case, the doubting of preparedness for the next stage and the struggle to recreate the acclaim elite athletes are used to receiving stems from a loss of the athlete's identity. Dr. Emma Vickers is a sports psychology doctor and the National Research Lead at the Talented Athlete Scholarship Scheme (TASS) based in the UK. The TASS is "a Sport England funded partnership between talented athletes, education institutions, and national governing bodies of sport. [The TASS] work[s] together to bring the best out of [the UK's] most exciting young talent. TASS helps athletes in

---

22 Emma Vickers, "LIFE AFTER SPORT: DEPRESSION IN THE RETIRED ATHLETE," Believe Perform (Blog), October 14, 2013.

education—aged 16-plus—to get the very best from their sporting and academic careers without having to choose between the two." In her research, Dr. Vickers has identified three main factors that drive mental health challenges for elite athletes post-retirement: "a loss of identity," "tunnel vision syndrome," and outside "biological factors."[23]

Dr. Vickers reiterates arguments from earlier in the book about the loss of identity driving many of the challenges faced and the correlation drawn in previous studies between identity association strength and the difficulty of the transition. Vickers cursorily addressed the concept of identity foreclosure when describing the "tunnel vision syndrome," writing, "Athletes who are unaware that they suffer from tunnel vision spend far too much time thinking only of training, competition, and results. As a result, athletes are left ill-prepared for the balanced perspective required of 'real world' career opportunities." She concludes by defending the idea both Conte and Leonard broached in their discussions on the subject, citing world-renowned peak-performance coach Bill Cole's work: "Athletes have had regular doses of serotonin daily for many years, when this is suddenly decreased or stopped outright, we see a huge upset to the chemistry of the body. A causal link between an imbalance in serotonin levels and depression has been explored by a number of researchers, however, more research in retired athletes posits exploration."[24]

***

---

23   Ibid.
24   Ibid.

The final academic study I'll cover in this chapter is one that provides a bit more clarity on the various types of transitions athletes may go through by applying personas to cover a broad population of transitions. In an article published in Qualitative Research in Sport titled "Adjusting to retirement from sport: narratives of former competitive rhythmic gymnasts," Cavallerio et. al surveyed and analyzed the post-athletic careers of former female gymnasts through a hybrid quantitative and anecdotal approach.[25] The article settles on the development of three primary narratives that encapsulate the post-retirement transition: the entangled narrative, the going forward narrative, and the making sense narrative. In each case, the persona is a former elite-level athlete who has recently retired from her sport and is dealing with the transition out of elite-level competition.

1. The Entangled Narrative: The entangled narrative tells the story of an athlete who has fiercely identified as an athlete for the majority of their cognitive life. This persona struggles to adapt to life without sport, realizing while they cannot return to life in their sport, they also do not know who they are without it. This persona struggles deeply with an inability to move forward and a desire to go back that creates a personal tension and sense of despair driven by the knowledge they must find a new identity but the uncertainty of determining how to do so.
2. The Going Forward Narrative: The going forward narrative is the antithesis of the entangled narrative. The going

---

25 Francesca Cavallerio et al., "Adjusting to retirement from sport: narratives of former competitive rhythmic gymnasts," *Qualitative Research in Sport, Exercise and Health*, 1-13, 2017.

forward persona identified as an elite athlete for much of their life, but also focused on developing identities and social circles outside of simply athletics. The transition of the going forward persona is smoother and lined with much less internal conflict than of the entangled narrative, and while they still identify in some ways with their athletic identity, they look back fondly on their memories of their career without yearning to return. The going forward narrative leverages the lessons learned from their time as an athlete as reasons for optimism for new passions and pursuits.

3. The Making Sense Narrative: The making sense narrative is the blend of the entangled and the going forward narratives. The persona, like the entangled and the going forward, spent most of their life building their athletic identity. They acknowledged there was a need to find an identity outside of their sport and attempted to find one with varying degrees of success. They look fondly upon their past success as an athlete with twinges of nostalgia but understand there's no going back and there are positive things to be gleaned from the experience. They deal with a great bit of uncertainty about what their future holds, but they sit somewhere in between the going-forward optimism and the entangled pessimism.[26]

These personas offer a lens through which to view the struggles of former athletes and even provide the opportunity for athletes to categorize themselves. While not exhaustive in nature, I believe these provide a structure with which we can

---

26 Ibid

more confidently classify the types of transitions athletes deal with when leaving their respective sport.

In speaking with former athletes and in my research, I've found myself yearning for more information on the subject of mental health and athletic retirement. As pointed out by Webb et. al, there is simply not enough empirical data to draw truly conclusive answers or insights on the psychological impact of retirement on the typical athlete.[27] However, what is lacking in empirical data is replete in anecdotal data. The plethora of athlete stories and opinions that describe a struggle that is both real and typical suggests that perhaps the data we do have, for now, doesn't tell the whole story and perhaps there is more to the struggle than meets the eye.

---

27   William M. Webb et al., "Athlete Identity and Reactions to Retirement from Sports," *Journal of Sport Behavior* 21, no. 3 (09, 1998): 338-362.

CHAPTER 4

A NEW VANTAGE POINT

So at this point you may be feeling as if I'm telling you a lot about the problem and not a whole lot about the solution—well, you'd be right.

My goal in the first part of this book is to try and educate and give context on a subject that has been, in my eyes, rather voiceless. I believe part of the struggle that occurs when transitioning out of highly competitive levels of athletics and the challenges that accompany it are due to a lack of conversation around the normalcy and the frequency of the athlete's struggle. In fact, prior to writing this book, I hadn't even disclosed much about the struggles I faced when I retired from football. But looking back now, based on my own experiences and trial-by-fire learning, I've realized putting structure around my transition and thinking through the event as a process would have made the experience a bit easier.

The truth is, I really didn't know what to expect when football and I parted ways.

The waves of emotional highs and lows, drastic changes to my day-to-day, and a lack of competitive outlets contributed to the sudden exposition that athletics had been the guardrails of my life. For a vast majority of my life, both consciously and subconsciously, I had been conditioned to certain disciplines and routines that provided a structure I wasn't even aware of—seasonal shifts in sport, early-morning weightlifting routines, social cues and responses to discipline and authority, and the playlist I listened to before every game, to name a few. Aspects of my personality and identity had been built within the playing field of these norms, and I was far from the only one.

***

Former NFL quarterback of fifteen years Trent Green explained as much in an interview with ESPN in 2012: "The hardest part is your daily routine. For 15 years, I knew exactly what I was doing in March, June and September because there was a schedule. When you take that away, you suddenly have a lot more time on your hands. I've been out of the game [for four years], and I still have a tough time with it. I find myself thinking, 'What's my motivation today?'"[28]

This lack of routine is a perfect example of the situation around the athlete, or the context of day-to-day life, providing insufficient structure in an athlete's transition. Viewed through a different, more theoretical lens, this failure of "situation" would be considered a deciding factor of the

---

28 Jeffri Chadiha, "Life after NFL a challenge for many," *ESPN.com*, May 31, 2012.

transition's success based on Nancy Schlossberg's transitional theory in her "4S System" of transitional success.[29]

Nancy Schlossberg, a world-renowned professor of sociology theory and counseling, theorized there are four main factors that support the success or failure of any transition event, defining a transition event as " [an event that] results in changes in relationships, routines, assumptions, and/or roles:" Situation, (Social) Support, Self, and Strategies.[30] In this theory, these four S's represent the major catalysts that enable either a positive or negative transition experience. The four S's can be understood as follows:

1. Situation is the milieu under which a transition occurs, whether or not the transition was a personal choice or circumstantial, the control you have over the transition, and the amount of change that comes with the transition, among many more contextual factors. The Situation is everything that is happening to you or around you during the transition process that may influence your decision-making or thought process.
2. Support, or Social Support, is the environment and the people who surround you during the period of your transition. It is your network of family, friends, institutions, communities, peers, and even strangers who can provide perspectives and comfort when called upon. Support requires the ability for you to trust your network to

---

[29] Nancy K. Schlossberg et al., *Counseling Adults in Transition Linking Practice With Theory*, New York: Springer, 1995.

[30] Ibid.

provide honest and open feedback and to be incorporated in your thinking and decision-making process.
3. Self is everything about you that could influence your decision-making—your socioeconomic status, your age, your health, your mood, your confidence, or your insecurity. Self is the factor that drives your outlook, be it optimism or pessimism, on the transition experience as a whole.
4. Strategies refers to the strategies you use to deal with the transition. Strategy effectiveness is evaluated by considering the type, the volume, and the quality of different approaches and coping mechanisms used during the transition experience.

The "4S System" provides a sociological framework through which we can evaluate the successes and failures of transitional experiences, so at this point, I think it's time to start with my own.

***

As mentioned before, I had a rather unceremonious end to my football career: the NFL was not going to be an option, and I had little desire to bother attempting to pursue a route the realist in me knew was a fruitless endeavor. So on a cold winter day in Upstate New York on November 19, 2016, when my teammates at Georgetown and I walked off the field at Colgate University after a perfunctory drubbing at the hands of the Red Raiders, I knew it would be the last time I suited up in a helmet and shoulder pads. There would be no advancement to the next level of competition for me.

Fast-forward roughly a year and a half or so, and I am no longer a student or a student-athlete, but a young professional working for a massive consultancy. I no longer have practices or weightlifting sessions early in the morning, but instead meetings, coffee chats, and conference calls. I go to the gym regularly, play the occasional round of golf or game of pick-up basketball, but serious athletics and competition have largely vanished from my day-to-day life. At this point, I am feeling a bit lost and uncomfortable in my "new normal," as the transition from athlete to former athlete has left me searching for something with which I can apply my passion for competition. Work is an outlet for many of the skills I gleaned along the journey of my athletic career, but I still do not have an outlet that meets what I really am looking for—a field of competition and a measuring stick.

On the scale that is my twenty-three years of life to that point, my time since football had ended was probably the most difficult year to date. I was in a funk that affected my moods, my outlook, and my day-to-day motivations. I found myself feeling like I was living for the weekends and spending the weekends chasing activities that didn't inspire passion or productivity. I was in a deep lull and wasn't sure how to start to climb out of it, telling myself it was just something that would pass—that is, until I found long-distance running.

My journey from retired college football player to marathoner began in January of 2018 in New York City, when on a non-hungover Saturday (sorry Mom, relatively rare back then) in the dead of winter, I decided to go for a run. At this point in my life, I was living on the West side of Manhattan, in a neighborhood called Hell's Kitchen, and was admittedly not much of a runner. In the time since I hung up my football cleats, I'd imagine I had gone for no more than ten runs, and none of them had been further than two miles. It had been almost a year since graduating college and over a year since my last snap of collegiate football.

On this cold January morning, I got up and decided for the first time in my life a run sounded nice, rather than a necessity. So off I went, aimlessly down the West Side Highway, first passing the ferry station and Chelsea Piers, with a frigid Hudson River accompanying me to my right. Ignoring the tracking feature of my watch for fear of the distance it would show, I looked up and saw the Freedom Tower standing a bit taller than the rest of the downtown Manhattan skyline. I decided it would make for a nice running landmark and made a mental note of my new destination. After what seemed like an eternity, I arrived at the Freedom Tower and the 9/11 memorial, wildly out of breath and legs shaking.

I took inventory of my organs to make sure everything was still there and checked my watch to see how far I had gone: 4.8 miles, without a shadow of a doubt the longest run of my life. Pride in my Herculean accomplishment lasted a few glorious seconds before realizing despite slaying the mental dragon that was this run, I had to find a way back to Hell's Kitchen. Given the state of my legs and central nervous system, I certainly was not going to run back. So I channeled my inner New Yorker and decided to bitch and moan as I begrudgingly walked back to my apartment. Little did I know at the time, but this run would be the turning point in my evolution as both an athlete and as a newfound non-athlete.

From that day on, I had a newfound sense of drive to improve upon my running prowess.

That run aside, I'd be remiss to ignore the impact my younger brother, Andrew, had on my journey into marathoning. A junior at USC and studying abroad in Hong Kong at the time, Andrew has always been a different breed: his singular drive and desire to be both excellent and unique in everything he does has long been an influence on me, even as his older brother. So when roughly around the same time as my Atlas-like effort down to the Freedom Tower, Andrew told me his New Year's resolution for 2018 was to run a marathon. I was both surprised and inspired. I told him if he was willing to do a marathon, I'd sign up for a half marathon with him, because in my own head "a marathon would be insane, but a half seems like a reasonable challenge for me," and thus the journey had officially begun. In July 2018, San Francisco, California, the Finnegan brothers would be taking on a new kind of opponent.

Within weeks, with my brother and I training concurrently across the globe, I realized my goal for a half marathon was not only achievable, but perhaps underwhelming by my own standards. By March, Andrew and I were sending our running stats to one another daily and had built an accountability system that allowed us to both grow closer and push ourselves further than we might have initially given ourselves credit for. This pushed me to change my registration and sign up for the full marathon.

Over the next three months, Andrew and I continued to train in our respective overpopulated cities and kept each other honest with our training, our diet, and our commitment to the race, constantly sharing our run data, sweaty selfies, and our introspective thoughts and feelings on how training was going for us both. We progressed in nonlinear fashions toward what the internet had told us was optimal marathon fitness and battled through blisters, loose toenails, hangovers, illnesses, one-hundred-hour work weeks and late school nights, injuries, and loads of self-doubt until race day finally arrived. There was almost nothing conventional about the days leading up to the race: Andrew and my family were flying in the day before from Los Angeles, and I was scheduled to meet them that same morning coming from an early flight out of Newark. I say scheduled because I did not in fact catch my original flight to Newark because I overslept and missed my flight.

I had stressed for six months about ensuring this weekend was a success and stressed accountability and discipline as the keys to my success, yet the only logistics I had to worry about prior to San Francisco were getting aboard that plane without turning an ankle, and I failed. Go figure. Thankfully, I caught another flight and made it to San Francisco in time for my race.

Today, the details of the race are a bit of a blur. I'd have a difficult time recalling any specific moment of the race with my brother save for hearing the gun go off, seeing my family at mile seventeen, repeatedly asking myself why I thought this was a good idea from mile twenty-two on, and the sheer exultation of crossing the finish line in under four hours after what felt like an eternity of a race. However, what I do remember with vivid detail is the moment when I rediscovered my gameday feeling–the-same feeling I've had before the first pitch of every baseball game or the jitters prior to the opening kick of any football game I've ever played in. It was a feeling I had been searching for ever since football retired from me, ever since the game I'd loved and adored since age six had left me at the altar and decided there wasn't another game for us to play. I found that same feeling I've always chased in a new hobby that asked me to do many of the same things football, and more broadly, sports had always asked me to do: sacrifice, grind, fight the mental and physical fatigue. I found the athlete I thought had been retired by his sport on a new field of play, and man, was he glad to be back.

***

If I take a look at my own story through the lens of the "4S System," it's clear to me I failed to approach my transition in any sort of a systematic plan. I was lacking in strategy, namely because I had none; I was lacking in self because I failed to acknowledge I would need to evaluate my own strengths and weaknesses; I failed in support because I leveraged no one in my family, friends, teammates, or network to help me through the struggle; and I failed in situation because I knew my career was coming to an end and I prepared myself for that with exactly zero proactive activities. I should have created a strategy that was centered around identifying what I loved about my time as a football player and the aspects of football that drove me to pursue it for sixteen years. I should have looked internally at myself and determined what my strengths and weaknesses were and how I could apply them outside of football. I should have spoken to my family, friends, former teammates, and anyone in my network who had successfully transitioned out of the sporting world to educate myself and heed their advice.

It should have come to no surprise to me the transition was challenging because truthfully, I treated it as an event that would work itself out rather than applying myself to ensure its success. To quote one of my favorite football coaches of all time, Coach Steve Grady from Loyola High School, "Hindsight's 20-20." In his case, he was usually using that saying to make a case to me the interception I had just thrown in practice would have been better served being thrown to one of my own receivers, but in this case it reminds me that looking back it should never have surprised me that I struggled to transition out of sports. Because I didn't prepare for it: I didn't even think to view my retirement from that vantage point.

Athletes know there are a million epigrams coaches love to float about the importance of practice: "Practice makes perfect," "Failure to prepare is preparing to fail," and "Success is when opportunity meets preparation," to name a few. But what I failed to realize at the time is by simply ignoring the transition and making no tangible effort to prepare for it, I failed myself on the back end.

***

Now, I think it's important to note not everyone will just find a new sport or a new hobby that will help fill the gap left by leaving athletics. So don't just go run a marathon and call me afterward if you don't feel the same way you did when you hit your first home run, scored your first goal, or dunked for the first time. There's no one-size-fits-all answer. But it is important to change the lens through which you may have to view the transition.

Ramona Shelburne, former Stanford softball outfielder and current senior writer and NBA Insider at ESPN, who we'll learn more about in a bit, said it best: "When you finish playing and when your athletic career is over, something that you've poured your heart and soul into and has been such a huge part of your identity—that part of yourself dies. That part of your career is over. It's like you're burying a part of yourself, and suddenly, instead of just a part of yourself, the part of yourself that gave you great self-confidence, great self-worth, a great sense of identity, a part of yourself that gave you all these great experiences, just feels like it's gone."

"But it's important to understand that even though it feels like that person is no longer there—it totally is. You totally are, you still are that person. The difference is you just can't be that person on the field anymore, and it takes time to view it that way."

Ramona's point is exactly what I hope to address in the next part of this book, to help change the way we as athletes view the next phase of life, and more importantly, to try and prevent others from making the same mistakes I and countless others have, blindly walking into an arena without practicing first.

CHAPTER 5

TALK ABOUT IT

At this point, you're probably asking yourself if you accidentally signed up for an educational textbook when you opened this thing up, rather than a nonfiction collection of stories with a couple of personal thoughts from a washed-up former athlete, and to this point, you'd be right. Prior to getting into any advice or observations and themes from my research and interviews, I wanted to ensure you, the reader, had the right context and were appropriately educated on what goes into the separation from an athlete and their sport. In the conversations I've been fortunate enough to have with various former high-level athletes across a variety of sports and experiences, as well as my own experiences, the difficulty transitioning from life with and without athletics is one that often is dealt with internally.

In a shocking revelation I'm sure no one could have anticipated, people tend to struggle with opening up and discussing their feelings and emotions. In fact, in talking with friends, family, former teammates, and other people I speak with regularly, almost none of them knew how much I struggled with my transition out of sport. No one knew I struggled to find motivation to work out, go out and hang with friends, or even anything beyond working, eating, and sleeping. For the vast majority of my first year or so after retirement, I found myself relatively listless for the first time in my life. I didn't feel like I had a tangible goal to work toward outside of work, and even that did not feel like it elicited the holistically best version of myself. Looking back now, if there's one obvious mistake I made in that period of time, it was deciding not to lean on the people I had around me.

As was discussed at length in last chapter's academic exploration of the sociological structure needed for a successful transition, social structure and support is one of the key aspects of a successful transition. In my case, I neglected the social support structure I would have needed to successfully transition my identity and caused myself many more headaches and difficult days because of it. With that in mind, the alternative way to handle the transition, and the first theme I'll highlight in the stories of athletes who have come out on the other side of the transition, is to "just talk about it."

Now what exactly does that mean? It means leaning on the people around you and in your life to support you before, during, and after your retirement and transition by talking to them, asking questions, and being honest about the things you're going through. It could be family, friends, teammates, colleagues, or people just generally in your network, but the common thread among athletes who feel as if they've successfully transitioned into the next phase of their life is they were active in surrounding themselves and engaging the people in their network about how to best move forward.

***

One of my favorite examples of this is a familiar subject, one Kobe Bean Bryant. Kobe Bryant was arguably the preeminent basketball player of the generation in which I was raised: from the late 1990s until the mid-2010s, Kobe the basketball player was widely considered as dominant a player, as ferocious a competitor, and as polarizing a figure as there was in all of organized athletics across the globe. Kobe transcended the sport of basketball with both his skill and competitive nature for two decades on the basketball court. His success on the court was well-documented and well-recognized. He also was an incredible student of the game, making a point as a young player in the league to pick the brains of NBA legends like Michael Jordan, Magic Johnson, and Larry Bird. Players who had succeeded at the highest levels and won championships—goals Kobe would insatiably pursue throughout his playing days.

Alas, even Kobe retired and had to hang up his sneakers in 2015. But what makes Kobe an interesting subject in the context of this discussion, however, is while one would assume Kobe's life after twenty years of playing at the highest level would still center on basketball, when Kobe finally retired, it did not. Instead, Kobe's life shifted into fields that on the surface did not fit the typical professional basketball player mold, spending his time on his venture capital firm, Bryant Stibel, his creative writing and storytelling in Dear Basketball and other children's books, and the creation of athletic leagues and training facilities such as the Mamba League and the Mamba Sports Academy. But how did Kobe end up in film, in venture capital, and in business in general? By leaning on his network, by leaning on his people.

What makes Kobe's path outside of basketball and as an athlete more interesting is while still very early in his career, he began to plot a path for his life after basketball. His journey for life after basketball began in 1999, at the age of twenty-one. It was at this point Kobe began to explore the world outside of sports by finding himself experts and legends in different industries to learn from, much in the same way he did with Michael, Magic, and Larry in basketball.

In one example, Kobe decided to head back to his childhood home of Italy for inspiration. "I was in Milan and wanted to meet with Giorgio Armani and talk to him a little bit about how he built his business," Bryant said, during his retirement press conference in 2015, of his time visiting the famous clothing designer back in 1999. "I said to myself, I'll probably play to 35, 36, whatever the case may be. He built a whole business at 40. What am I going to do with the rest of my life? What comes next?"[31]

Kobe's pursuit of information and learning did not stop there at twenty-one, however: he continued to hunt information and actively find access to educational opportunities. His pursuits extended as far as Hollywood, speaking with film

---

31 Sam Amick, "Kobe Bryant finds 'Muse' beyond basketball artistry," *USA Today*, Feb. 25, 2015.

luminaries such as Steven Spielberg, J.J. Abrams, John Williams, Mark Parker, and Jony Ive, to name a few.[32]

"I'll just cold call people, absolutely." Kobe explained in a 2016 interview with ABC.[33]

"I'll just cold call people and pick their brain about stuff. Some of the questions that I'll ask will seem really, really simple and stupid, quite honestly, for them. But if I don't know, I don't know. You have to ask. I'll just do that. I'll just ask questions and I want to know more about how they build their businesses and how they run their companies and how they see the world."[34]

Kobe's insistence on finding out as much information about how people successful outside of sports achieved and sustained success and his ability to translate that into his own satisfaction and fulfillment is probably the standard bearer of successful transitions. So much so Chris Conte, former NFL defensive back who we had the chance to learn more about earlier, even referenced Kobe as an example for others athletes to aspire to, saying, "I think a really good example of [a successful transition] was Kobe Bryant and how he seamlessly transitioned and how all-in he was on working with his daughter and his philanthropies and the other things that he was doing." Kobe's transition was so seamless, albeit only a

---

32   Associated Press, "Kobe Bryant bouncing film ideas off Spielberg, Abrams, Bruckheimer," ESPN.Com, May 20, 2016.
33   Tony Manfred, "Kobe Bryant Cold Calls Business People To Ask Them Questions About How To Be Successful," Business Insider, Jul. 22, 2014.
34   Ibid.

public perception of a frictionless transition, that he inspired other athletes in the pursuit of a similarly smooth transition.

While Kobe was certainly the most famous example of knowing how to leverage your network and lean on your people, he's undoubtedly not the only former athlete to succeed in part by leaning on others for inspirations. In fact, of the dozens of people I spoke to, interviewed, surveyed, and researched, time and time again a recurring theme of successful transition was the ability to lean on the people within their network to figure out how to move forward and find their next channel.

***

Marina Paul, as you may remember from earlier in our story, is a former standout defender for the Georgetown University women's soccer team. A multiple-time All-Big East selection as a defender for the Hoyas, Marina's career at Georgetown was nothing short of spectacular. Leaving the Hilltop, as Georgetown is affectionately referred to, as the captain of the first Georgetown women's soccer team to ever have won a Big East title and the first team in program history to advance to the NCAA Women's Soccer College Cup Final Four.

Marina's career was an objective success on and off the field, as she also excelled in the classroom and professionally, garnering a number of internships during college and graduating from school with both a bachelor's from the McDonough School of Business and a master's in integrated marketing communications. Marina is a standard bearer for the quintessential student-athlete, dedicated to both her sport and life outside of it, but even she admitted the transition into retirement hit her harder than expected.

"Oh, I'm chilling, this is fine," Marina divulged about her first venture into life without sports.

> "I'll find a hobby or something to do. I love sports. I'll still play [from time to time]. I didn't want to go play professionally. I was over it. I wanted to use my brain. And then I just crashed because I tried to place so many fillers in my life, but it was so unfulfilling trying to create structure, and I didn't know how to do it. I think we are so conditioned to have coaches tell us what to do all the time. When that was gone, I had to even figure out what to do on the weekends, I literally just froze, like what am I supposed to do? I'd think, Go to the beach volleyball courts at Lincoln and I'd be there for like seven hours because I didn't know where else to be. And I didn't feel like I fit in with the rest of the world culture."

But as one would expect, when an athlete like Marina was put in a corner by her situation, like any competitive athlete, she was determined to find her way out of it and back on top by any means necessary, including asking for help. So when she reached her most challenging point, Marina leveraged her network and began looking for support, starting with friends and teammates and eventually ending up on a Greyhound bus headed back to Georgetown, looking for inspiration and reinforcement in the office of the athletic director.

> "When I was in my deepest hole, I took a bus down from New York to DC and reached out to [Lee Reed,

> Georgetown athletic director] and asked, 'Can we meet up?' and ended up meeting with him for a couple hours. He told me about his career and how hard the transition was for him [Mr. Reed was a basketball player himself at Cleveland State] and why he still works in sports now, because he tried to transition out and hated it. So I talked to him about how important it would be to have, like, this group of alumni to be resources for them to reach out as a networking resource."

Crediting this as a pivotal point in her transitioning experience, Marina set back out with a more structured approach and a sense of confidence she too would turn the corner and find an outlet, and finally she did.

Cut Seven is a training center in Washington, DC, that lists itself on its website as "NOT A GYM. A TEAM," and Cut Seven is where Marina found what she had been missing most: an outlet for the athlete within. "This community where I started going [Cut Seven] because one of the founders played college football at UConn, and he was just awesome. Everything about it, the way they operate, the way they talk, was exactly what I was looking for. I had an epiphany, like, 'Oh, he like runs it like it's like preseason,' which was super familiar and some of the athletic minutiae that I was definitely missing."

Since joining Cut Seven, Marina noted how much better she's felt feeling like she has her own team again: "It's been a really cool community to be in. That's all where all my friends are from, and we do everything together now, but the biggest thing was just finding my team again, because it was definitely out there."

***

Some athletes believe so much in the value of a supporting network to go so far as to dedicate their life and profession to providing the infrastructure of support networks for other athletes who are going through their own transitions.

Meet Myriam Glez.

A two-time Olympic synchronized swimmer for both France and Australia. Myriam's own athletic journey spanned multiple countries, multiple continents, and multiple retirements over the span of a three-decade career as an athlete, a coach, and an administrator.

> *"I started synchronized swimming when I was six years old. I actually saw it on TV for the first time at the European Championship and then eventually saw it in the Olympics, but I really saw it on TV and that's how I decided to start and got into a local club."*

Born and raised in France, a young Myriam was immediately hooked on the sport, committing to a regimented training program five days a week at just seven years old. Her potential and progress were evident to anyone with a cursory understanding of the sport, and by nine years old she was competing in groups with athletes several years older than her. However, Myriam had dreams and plans much larger than most nine-year-olds.

> "Even at ten years old, I had already shared with my parents and coaches, and really any of the people around me who'd listen, that I wanted to be on the national team and that I was going to be in the Olympics one day."

Ten-year-old Myriam would turn out to be quite prescient, moving up the age ranks quickly and eventually competing in and winning championships both domestic and abroad as a teenager. Her early success and long-term potential eventually led the French Olympic Committee to take notice, and it suggested she make swimming her number-one priority by dropping out of her standard school and moving to Paris.

> "I dropped out of middle school and moved to the National Training Center in Paris. Which was effectively the National Training Center for athletes [in addition to schooling]—so if you want to compete at the highest level, and if you're not already on a professional team, like in soccer or rugby, you basically go to that training center."

> "So, I moved there when I was fifteen, in 1994, which was pretty early. And then pretty soon, in 1997, I was on the highest-level national team and I was training for contention on the Olympics squad for 2000 and eventually competed with the French team in the 2000 Sydney Olympics. So, I competed with the team from '97 on and was on the national team from '94 to 2003."

> "So like a good ten years of competing at the at the highest level for my country."

Shortly after the Sydney Olympics, Myriam started to consider what she wanted her life to look like when she could no longer compete in her sport and began exploring her options to pursue an MBA. She nailed her exams and was accepted into one of the top MBA programs in Europe, all while training for the 2004 Athens Olympics. However, much to her dismay, the French Olympic Committee considered competing and pursuing an MBA mutually exclusive decisions and asked her to pick one or the other.

Myriam was forced into her first retirement, as she believed the opportunity to get her degree was just too important to pass up and the school wouldn't provide another chance at application if she turned down their offer of admission.

"That was a pretty rough moment. It was my first retirement, and at the point I thought that would be it and I was pretty bitter about having to choose between school and sport. It was compounded especially because my school was willing to be flexible about the schooling and the years it would take and allow me to just take a few classes every year if needed [so long as I attended]."

Despite her rough transition and breakup with the sport, Myriam managed to find academic and professional success in her MBA pursuit and professional transition working for a hotel company that took her all around the globe, until she landed back in Australia, where she had first achieved her Olympic aspirations. It was in Sydney where Myriam's athletic journey, and ultimately her professional one, was rerouted permanently.

> "It was maybe two, three years after retiring, and I was now in Australia—I didn't know anybody and I was trying to figure out how to socialize and meet people. And all I could think of was trying to go back to the sport to see if I could meet some people with the same interests.
>
> "Sure enough, I contacted the Federation and let them know I was looking to coach. They didn't have a national club at the time, but they invited me to a national competition to actually compete! I actually went and participated in the national championship. But I had been retired and traveling and partying a bit, completely out of real training, so then I was really walking into the competition totally unprepared. But I ended up winning! The level in Australia was pretty low at the time in comparison to Europe, but it was a ton of fun."

The competition wound up acting as a springboard for Myriam's second act as an Olympic athlete, as she was able to gain Australian citizenship and jump-start the Australian program, competing in the 2008 Beijing Olympics, all while keeping her job working at the hotel company. Her swimming "second wind" provided some of the athletic closure she had been seeking since her departure from the French program, ultimately leading her into her second retirement, this time on her own terms.

Myriam transitioned into coaching. Working with the English synchronized swimming team in London before ultimately moving to the US, where she became the high performance director for the USA synchronized swimming team and finally the CEO of the US program.

At this point, having spent six years working with and leading the US team, Myriam decided to expand her influence to reach more athletes in a formal coaching role, founding Athletes Soul—a company whose mission is to "support and serve the interests of athletes as they transition out of sports and raise awareness about the challenges of athletic retirement."

> *"Athletes Soul really came out of me helping quite a few of my former athletes that I had coached through their retirement and realizing that there wasn't a lot formal support available to them at the time. In the course of my career, I ended up meeting quite a lot of athletes, and as I was going through the process of, like, researching what was available and how to help athletes and we just felt that we could create something that wasn't dependent on a sporting organization and offer something that was like a peer-to-peer system to support athletes through the transition—that that could be most helpful."*

"Getting people to talk through their transition was so important for me and for my athletes; I just thought that a formal program could help a lot of athletes too."

***

Kobe, Marina, and Myriam took very different paths to finding fulfillment again after the end of their athletic days. Kobe sought to find different passions while still in the midst of his athletic career. Marina made a point to stay focused on her athletic career while she was still in it, noting she knew it would be a finite period of time and wanted to make the most of it. Myriam found her passion in Athletes Soul only through the rough "education" she received in her own retirement experiences.

However, all three athletes found their own passions and outlets in part because of their willingness to open up and seek support, information, and advice from the people in their network. Myriam, Marina, and Kobe all demonstrated a willingness to ask for help and seek the support they needed to ease the burden of their transition.

Marina even went so far as to offer advice for future athletes who may find themselves in similar situations:

"Everyone will struggle in their own way, which is a bummer because that's just how it is for a period of time. But I also want to emphasize it's not weak or shameful to ask for help. I was able to lean on my friends and teammates and other people in my [social] circle for support, and they helped me through it."

If there's one takeaway from these stories, it's this: whether you are trying to preempt your transition or just get through it, it doesn't have to fall on your shoulders to figure it all out. Lean on others instead, and don't be afraid to talk about it.

CHAPTER 6

WHY YOU REALLY PLAYED

―――

If being willing to lean on your people and talk about it requires you to look externally for support, this next piece of advice will request you look inward to ease your own transition. "Why you really played" is an overly simplified direction to ask you to take a hard look about what it is you actually love about your sport and work to seek those same things out in any other field, hobby, or passion you decide to venture into. In every interview I've done with the score of former athletes, I've asked the question in some way, shape, or form, "What is or was your favorite aspect of your sport?"

I asked this not hoping to learn that Anthony Perasso, our rowing friend from Boston College, really loved the feeling of extraordinary muscular strain tugging seven other large men in a boat across various bodies of water—which to be fair, wasn't his answer—but to figure out what the common themes were among athletes when asking them to be really introspective about why they loved playing their sports.

In fairness to Perasso, his real answer, not the one I fabricated for the purposes of drawing this dichotomy, was a bit more thoughtful.

"My favorite part is that sports teach you the value of hard work: the value of recognizing that something may take months or years to complete, but if you put your head down and grind for it you are going to get there." Perasso's introspective approach led him to realize things he loved the most about his sport weren't even the activities that made it a sport, but rather the process by which he attained success in his sport.

When applying this frame of mind to the transition experience of leaving athletics behind, it is important to recognize there is a difference between enjoying the activity of your sport, playing the sport itself, and the characteristics of the sport that really drive your love for it—everything it has provided you and taught you kept you pursuing success within its confines.

If you can recognize the underlying qualities and characteristics your sport provided you with while playing as an athlete, you can learn to seek those same qualities and characteristics outside of the sport itself.

For some, this may mean identifying the process to reach success is what drives you, which is exactly the case that Perasso identified for himself, who now spends a great deal of his free time writing and working on creating projects.

> "My passion—call it writing—the process is basically to stare at a blank sheet and see what happens, while knowing that it's going to take a while. In the end, maybe it'll be good, maybe it'll suck, but you have to do the work to find out. That [was] rowing. Rowing is like hours and hours of practice for six minutes of race, so you learn you just have to shut up and do the work and trust the process, even though you can't see the light at the end of the tunnel, something that I find in writing too."

***

For others, identifying the things you love the most about what your sport provided you with can lead to the creation of a new passion for yourself altogether. Michael Chabala, the former MLS player who we met earlier in Chapter two, reached the end of his MLS career in 2014.

After a series of harsh realities, team roster shenanigans, and reneged promises from front-office members and coaching staffs, Chabala was confronted with the painful fact his soccer career was coming to a close. Faced with the prospects of life without soccer, Michael worked a variety of jobs and career paths looking for something to reignite his passion and fill the hole that the end of his athletic career had created to no avail.

With minimal support from the MLS and his former employing teams, Michael began what he described as "a search for fitness that would be equivalent to what I was used to as a professional athlete—and at this point there was nothing close to it." At this point in his search for the next chapter,

Chabala began to consider what he missed most about his playing days—a sense of team, a camaraderie, and as mentioned, the fitness. Lo and behold, a business and a passion were born.

Sphere's website describes the soccer-inspired fitness boutique as "[a way] to recreate the locker room [Chabala] missed and offer an endurance-based team concept that gave the general fitness community a taste of soccer-inspired fitness."[35] But Chabala explains it's much more than that.

"I wanted to help guys; I wanted to create a business that would help other players. I wanted them to not have to struggle like I did, to create an opportunity by creating a business that will help them create businesses," Chabala said of the inspiration that helped him create Sphere.

Sphere is a US-based fitness start-up that offers a variety of classes ranging from indoor mini-ball soccer classes to high-intensity interval training and core workouts, both in person and online. Founded in 2015 in the parking lot of an optometry office and since expanded to facilities and franchises across the country, Sphere was the brainchild of Chabala in search for a way to combine his love of soccer, fitness, and to replace the locker room—his favorite part of playing soccer. Chabala and his team of "coaches," oftentimes former athletes and soccer players themselves, teach classes centered around hybrid soccer concepts and fitness classes that promote a challenging, push-yourself workout that begs the best of its participants. But Sphere, and Chabala

---

35 Michael Chabala, "Our Story," Sphere.Club, accessed May 6, 2020.

by extension, have also really found, fostered, and developed a new locker room and a new community unlike any other.

"Sphere is an extension of what I believe a locker room should have looked like, where everyone loves each other regardless of style of play, position on the field—truly being bought in to one team and one idea."

Based in Houston and franchised across other cities in Texas and the US, Sphere's "locker room" is composed of former athletes and non-athletes alike, giving Chabala and other retired athletes a community with both similar and different perspectives on fitness, business, and life in general. Giving his coaches a way to stay connected to their sport and their favorite aspects of it.

What has made Chabala successful in his transition from a professional soccer player to a fitness start-up entrepreneur was his ability to look inward and determine what soccer provided him that he deemed most important. For Chabala, Sphere is simply an extension of the fact the locker room soccer provided him from his days in Austria as an eight-year-old until his retirement at thirty was the driving source of his love of the game and the experience. So much so he invested all of himself and his energy into recreating that locker room for a larger community.

***

While some athletes will have to spend significant time and commitment to ultimately discovering, sometimes it is possible to find a new outlet that parallels your sport simply by circumstance.

Mary Ricks is the president of Kennedy Wilson, a publicly traded real estate company headquartered in Beverly Hills, California, that manages nearly 18 billion dollars' worth of real estate assets. Mary is also a former two-time NCAA softball champion and four-year varsity starter in center field for the UCLA Bruins, and she believes both of those facts are directly correlated to one another. The youngest of four children who would end up playing collegiate Division 1 athletics, Ricks' adolescence and young-adult life were always dominated by sports.

> *"I was the youngest of four kids, my oldest brother went to 'SC [USC] and played baseball for Rod Deadeaux [Hall of Fame baseball coach for USC] on a baseball scholarship. My sister went to UNLV and she was on a basketball scholarship, and since became a college head coach. My whole family was just all about sports. And so right from the time I could walk, I was running around and competing with them and trying to play with them and keep up with them."*

Mary's athletic background and family helped mold her into a burgeoning softball star—so much so when she arrived at UCLA for her freshman year, she was immediately ready to make an impact.

> *"I went to UCLA and I started as a freshman. I felt just super lucky that I was able to even be there. I remember first going to school and starting to practice with the team,*

and we had some of the best players in all of them in softball, some of whom went on to play Olympic softball and win gold medals, and just being on a team with that kind of talent, I was just awestruck when I was that young. It was the first time I'd ever been away from home, and there I was playing ball with these athletes who were just incredible, and on top of that, then, that they all sort of took me under their wing."

Despite that initial feeling of awe, Mary was an immediate contributor to the squad during her freshman year, batting second and manning center field for the Bruins on a team who Mary described as "the best team I was on in [my] four years," stifled only by a case of the flu that infected twelve of the fourteen team members the night before the semifinals.

"I'll never forget Dottie Richardson, who played shortstop for us and wound up a two-time Olympic gold medalist. First at bat of the semifinal, Dottie gets up, rips the ball into left center, dives into second base, raises her hands to call time out, waves over the trainer to come out, and the trainer comes out with a bucket [into which Dottie lost her lunch]."

Despite her freshman year aspirations being derailed by a virus (might sound familiar to some of you current athletes reading this in the post-2020 world), Ricks and the Bruins went on to win back-to-back NCAA titles the following years, establishing UCLA as the preeminent women's softball power of the 1980s. However, once her softball career began to wind to a close and her senior season had arrived, Ricks had come to grips with the fact she wasn't planning on pursuing a professional career in softball.

> "I was not sure if I wanted to really end my playing career, and a lot of my teammates had gone on to play [professionally] and onto play in the Olympics. But I think just a commitment that you need to have to do that if you got to be all in. So, I was ready to move into, you know, a working career. I just couldn't figure out how to play softball at the level that you need to play to play in the Olympics; I couldn't figure that out. So yeah, it was time to move on. And it was hard, it was definitely super hard to leave."

At this point in her life, Ricks "stumbled" into an opportunity that would prove to eventually provide her with her competitive outlet for softball, business, and more specifically real estate.

> "I owe it to athletics really, because the recruiter for this firm was a former UCLA athlete. He went to Dr. Judy Holland, who was an athletic director at the time, and he asked her if she had to have any 'graduating seniors who [are] competitive and [that] you would recommend? We have one slot open.' And Dr. Holland recommended me. So I was super lucky that she did that. And I didn't know anything about real estate, nothing. But you know, the recruiter, Larry Miller [told me], 'You don't have to know anything about real estate. Just come on board. We'll teach you everything.' I just lucked into the job and I ended up loving it."

Mary found she had a natural propensity for the inherent competition in business and even the most challenging and occasionally mundane projects would get her competitive juices flowing. "In that junior training program, I was obviously the only young woman back then because the program was almost all young guys, and we would be asked to do things like cold calling in the evenings. So my boss would have these contests and he would say, 'We're gonna do a cold-calling contest: whoever can make the most initial appointments,' and he'd always pull out like, a one-hundred-dollar bill from his pocket, '... you get the one-hundred-dollar bill.' And for me it wasn't about the hundred-dollar bill. It was a game, right? And I was playing that game and I was going to beat everyone that I was playing with. It was all in fun, of course, but oh my gosh, we all went at it so hard."

"I was going to beat everyone that I was playing with."

Ignoring Mary's evident athletic talent and business acumen for a second, it's clear in the repeated quote above a component of what drove her to success both in sport and in business was her inherent love of competition and her unrelenting desire to achieve success. But even more than that, understanding her love of competition was part of her love of sport allowed her to successfully transition from the softball diamond to the meeting room.

"Getting the competitiveness going for me and allowed me to vent all out on a daily basis was huge. It gave me a way to feel like I was back playing again."

***

You may be wondering why in a chapter discussing the importance of self-reflection, I just highlighted three examples of former athletes who seemed to have conflicting experiences of self-reflection in pursuit of their next passions. Well, the reality is, there's no perfect way to handle this aspect of transitioning.

- Chabala had his back to the wall and was actively looking for ways to keep soccer in his life when he founded Sphere and decided his transition would be marked by the things he loved most about soccer and providing an opportunity for other former players to have a smoother transition than he did.
- Perasso loved the process of success in crew and found outlets that demanded similar levels of mental toughness and grind.
- Ricks is and was hyper-competitive and found success in the real estate world brought her similar levels of intensity and drive that softball had previously provided.

The common thread among these three athletes, who vary in age, demographic, level of competition, and post-athletic outlet, is each eventually realized their outlet had to include something they also found in sport. So the advice gleaned from these stories is simple—figuring out what you love about your sport on the front end will save you pain and time on the back end. If you know what about your sport makes you tick, and why you really played for as long as you did, it will be easier to find things that can satisfy those aspects of sport when it's time to hang 'em up.

CHAPTER 7

FIND A NEW TEAM

When I ask athletes what the one thing they miss the most about their sport is during our interviews and surveys, the number one answer, probably upward of 75 percent of all answers, is they miss the locker room. The locker room, in this case, isn't a physical location or somewhere with folding chairs and a place for a backpack, but rather the intangible feeling and environment that is cultivated by a camaraderie athletics foster. The locker room represents a chaotic sanctuary that allows for lifelong bonds and friendships, open conversations of learning and disagreement, physical and verbal altercations, and more jokes than the West Village on a Saturday night.

It is a place where athletes often feel like they can be themselves and explore their personalities with peers of similar mindsets and oftentimes different backgrounds. Truth be told, the locker room is the thing I miss the most about athletics to this day. I miss the shared laughs, conversations, arguments, concerts, and stand-up comedy shows that seemed to take place on a daily basis. So when an athlete tells me this is the piece of sports they miss the most, I'm not surprised because that loss is a part of being an athlete that goes without saying to other athletes. We all get it. However, what most people and athletes fail to recognize, or even acknowledge, is finding your next locker room is also a key part of the success in transitioning. The key to finding your next locker room is being open to actively trying new things.

Many of the athletes I've spoken to have described to me they simply didn't know what to do with themselves when they retired. They weren't sure whether or not they'd be able to replace their sport with a hobby or whether they would feel adequately fulfilled by a new job or new endeavor. So many go back to what they've always done—training regimens similar to ones they were asked to do as athletes, albeit at a lower level of intensity, and a hodge-podge of informal attempts at various recreational sports. What these efforts fail to acknowledge when they appear to fall flat is it often is not the sport itself or even the activities that define it that causes the unfulfilling nature, but the lack of a team environment around them that does. Athletics in general are built around support systems that drive an athlete to success, and be it teammates, coaches, or trainers, all athletes have some form of a social environment around them that allows them to flourish and grow. When an athlete leaves their sport behind, that support system often disappears.

In researching and learning about how different athletes from various sports and levels have handled their transitions, one thing that has seemed to show up time and time again is the ability to find a new team is a driver of success. Much like how Michael Chabala, the former Houston Dynamo and MLS veteran, decided upon retirement it was his mission to create his own new team by founding his company Sphere, or like Marina Paul, our former captain of the Georgetown women's soccer team, who managed to find her team with the Cut Seven gym, athletes who have found successful transitions have seemed to find teams in a variety of ventures, hobbies, and activities.

So how did these athletes find their new teams, their new locker rooms? To put it bluntly, they tried and failed at a whole bunch of other things first. They picked up new hobbies, put them back down, and picked up ones not even tangentially related. For me, I tried everything, from boxing to pick-up basketball to slow-pitch softball, before I found the running and endurance racing community was the new team for me. Others are able to find their new teams in other avenues, sometimes even at work.

***

Kodi Whitfield is a former standout football player at Stanford University and a high school teammate of mine at Loyola down in Los Angeles, California. A highly decorated high school football recruit, Kodi was recognized as a top-twenty wide receiver prospect in the entire country and a top-fifty recruit in all of California, starring on both sides of the football for Loyola. Arriving at Stanford in the fall of 2012, immediately forced his way onto the field, playing in thirteen of fourteen games for the Cardinal. But it was his sophomore year that proved most noteworthy for Kodi, as he started at wide receiver and played in every game, even landing on ESPN and SportsCenter's weekly Top 10 Plays for his jaw-dropping one-handed touchdown reception against UCLA in Stanford Stadium.

However, after his sophomore season, his coaches asked Kodi to transition to the other side of the football and play safety for the Cardinal. At this point was when Kodi first started to consider professional football may not have been in the cards for him: "It became pretty apparent, especially once I switched positions, that it was going to take a damn good effort and a damn good season to make it [to the NFL] given that I was moving from receiver to safety. And I think as you know, the production on the field became what it was, the playing time became what it was, and it became pretty apparent what my career in football is going to look like." As Kodi alluded to, his transition to safety was a success in that he was both productive and successful for Stanford in his two years on defense, but not quite successful enough to pursue the NFL, in his own opinion, in earnest.

At this point, for the first time in his athletic career, Kodi wasn't certain what was next. "I think I never really knew what a career outside of football was going to look like until the plug on football was basically pulled," Kodi explained. "I had to address it with myself: 'You know, there is no going with the flow [anymore]. There is no just showing up to practice and seeing what happens anymore. That is literally gone,' and that is when I was finally forced to think, 'Who is Kodi Whitfield outside of the white lines?'"

A product engineering major at Stanford, he thought perhaps that would be a field in which he could pursue a career outside of football, and so, in part to buy himself a bit more time,

Kodi went to acquire a masters at Oregon University focused on sports-related product design. Despite feeling like he was ready to move on from high-level football, when he arrived at Oregon, Kodi decided to jump at the chance to hop on the field again, playing flag football in a local recreational league. "There is no right answer, but find what works for you. And if anything, try it all. Try coaching a high school team. Maybe even volunteer to play flag football," Kodi said. "Getting out that energy, getting out there and reminding yourself of that excitement that you had for the game and the excitement you get from competing. Just try things."

Kodi's willingness to try things and get out there has also paid off in finding his new team—his core group of fellow product engineers at Adidas, many of whom he's found have similar interests and backgrounds as he does. "One of my teammates at Adidas played college football at Oregon, is from Los Angeles, went to Culver City High School, and has this crazy similar track and route as me, and we both end up here—it's crazy! You start to realize the value of mentors and you just remember what it's like to be able to go to upperclassmen and really have them take you under their wing while adjusting to the change: it's like finding a new locker room."

When asked for the key to success in finding a new team, Kodi offered a poignant parting thought: "You definitely have to go searching, maybe a little high and low, for it. It's like being back on the playground again: you want to go hang out on the basketball courts, because you like playing basketball and you find people who like the same thing you do. So it's navigating life that way and immersing yourself among the different groups to maybe find a group that you just click with. But again, it's just smaller. So where I had maybe twenty 'ride or dies' on the football team, but you're cool with all one hundred of them, now I've got maybe twenty guys on my entire [working] team, but I'm coolest with four who I consider my real squad."

Kodi's approach to life after football was centered on surrounding himself with like-minded people and "teammates" he could rely on to navigate the transition. He identified he wanted a support system around him and found a team who mimicked his locker room. While Kodi was able to find his team by seeking out similar people in the environments around him, many others have found their new teams by approaching even their trial-and-error phase with the same structure that defined their athletic careers.

***

Max Browne is a former University of Southern California quarterback and team captain and spent a year as the starter at the University of Pittsburgh as a graduate transfer. Even in our interview, Max's approach and passion with which he attacked the questions was both impressive, inspiring, and obvious: his ability to demand excellence of himself and others makes it no surprise he has done so well in his time after athletics, nor does it come as a surprise his advice is so profound.

For those of you who aren't college football aficionados, the name Max Browne may not ring a bell immediately. But for those of you who are, you know Max Browne's collegiate football story is about as intriguing as they come. Max's time in the limelight began as a five-star quarterback recruit, the highest such ranking high school and college football recruiting services offer, and the number-one-ranked high school quarterback in the country in 2012 as the starting quarterback for Skyline High School, which Max described as "a serious football school" in Sammamish, Washington. The two-time Washington State player of the year would win three high school state titles in his illustrious career before he headed off to the University of Southern California (USC), a prestigious football school known for delivering high-talent football players to the NFL, to begin what would almost assuredly be the next stepping stone on his way to the NFL. Until it wasn't.

Browne waited in line, so to speak, to be the next great USC quarterback for his first three years on campus, sitting behind future NFL quarterback Cody Kessler and finally, in 2016, winning the starting job coming out of training camp and even being named team captain for the Trojans. His time to shine had arrived. However, the 2016 season did not start off well for the Trojans, as they lost two of their first three games, games in which Max played in serviceable fashion, but not up to his own exceedingly high standards, nor those of the national media or his coaching staff.

He was "getting creamed by the national media," and by the fourth game, Max was replaced by a redshirt freshman named Sam Darnold, and the rest was history. Darnold, who Max described as "arguably the most talented quarterback in the history of USC," proceeded to go on a historic tear, helping USC turn their season around en route to an end-of-year Rose Bowl victory over Penn State. Sam's success continued the next year, and he was promptly drafted third overall in the 2018 NFL draft.

All the while, Max was put in the unenviable position of dealing with the public backlash of his shortcomings on the field, made more noticeable by the successes of Darnold. However, something that remains true to this day, as I learned while interviewing him, is Max has a special talent for "blocking out the noise" and grinding regardless of the circumstances out of his control.

Max continued to work behind the scenes and in practice, ready and waiting, ensuring he was prepared for his next opportunity. At the end of the 2016 season, Browne used his final year of NCAA eligibility to transfer to the University of Pittsburgh to try and rewrite the script on his collegiate career. Max, in his exceeding humility, would likely disagree, but a combination of bad luck and injury robbed him of that opportunity, and his collegiate career came to a close. After rehabbing his injury and a final attempt to make an NFL roster during workouts with the Pittsburgh Steelers and Washington Redskins didn't go as planned, Max decided to end his football pursuits.

However, at this point, Max's story gets particularly interesting. Labeled a "bust" because his football career hadn't panned out how the media and fanbases had expected it to, Browne was left looking for the next chapter—something to make him tick outside of football, looking for a new team.

"I moved to the other side of the country, took a minimum-wage job, and not just to say I did it, but to work for a guy that I wanted to learn from, [Gary Vaynerchuk]." Max decided the best way to find his new team was to move from Los Angeles to New York and work for entrepreneur Gary Vaynerchuk.

"I wanted to be part of his ecosystem. I didn't have any idea what I wanted to do. I had all these degrees, but no idea what I wanted to do. And I said, screw it. I'm gonna go work for this guy."

Max worked for Vaynerchuk for a year, parlaying a minimum-wage job and the experiences that accompanied learning from someone he admired into a new passion and line of work as a sports broadcaster, doing work for USC, ABC, and the PAC-12 athletic conference radio program on Sirius XM.

However, what struck me most during my conversation with Max was his inspiring message on what his advice would be to athletes who are looking for the next chapter: "You have got to go out and taste things; you have got to go out and find what you like. I think athletes struggle finding what they want to do in life because they're so locked into their sport. And so, I would say flip the script, find someone you want to be like, find someone you want to work for, and screw the exact job or position title or whatnot.

Go find the human being that you're like, 'Hey, I'd love to live his life and be like him in twenty years, ten years, fifteen years.' Go work for that person, try to get in their ecosystem, try to get in there in their network and do whatever it takes to get in there. I think life has windows of opportunity, and that opportunity, right when you start playing sports, before you get kids and wife and all that, or spouse—that's an invaluable opportunity to go make some moves and test some things."

***

Max and Kodi's ability to transition successfully was driven by their willingness and comfort in trying new things and focusing on the process instead of concerning themselves with the outcome. Both he and Kodi made points to identify the things they were looking for in their transitions and what was missing in the next phases of life for them and pursued them, ignoring the risk of failure. Neither Kodi nor Max was afraid to take a risk and put everything on the line in search of a new team, and that dedication and importance of finding that new team is what the main takeaway from this chapter should be. It's often overlooked how devastating the loss of a locker room can be on an athlete's psyche—losing the network around you that you've grown accustomed to seeing daily is a massive transition to undergo for anyone—and because of that, it's vital to find your new team and to create your own new locker room.

CHAPTER 8

GEAR UP LIKE GAME DAY

One of the most difficult parts of the typical athlete transitioning experience is figuring out where and how to begin to move on. For the vast majority of an athlete's athletic career, you are told what to do, where to be, when to be there, and how it will help move you along in your pursuit of success.

You are told showing up at 6 a.m. at the campus or team's weight room (which really means 5:55 a.m., but that's a whole different can of worms), lifting these weights this many times with this form, and doing so frequently will make you stronger and thus better at your sport in these ways. You're told if you do these things on the court, play this way on the pitch, and make these throws on the field, you'll demonstrate enough ability to continue to advance and move up the competitive ladder. An athletics journey has structure that simply does not exist in any other institution.

So after all of the years of your career, you're simply expected to "figure it out," a meaningful chasm is created in your day-to-day routine. Where there used to be structure and sometimes constraint, there is now an open world of possibilities... and quite a bit of uncertainty.

Former standout Georgetown University women's volleyball captain Ashlie Williams explained to me that even the routine you develop as an athlete is empowering and losing it upon retirement feels like a slap in the face.

> "I really missed the structure it had given my life. Because I was spending so much time playing sports, it felt like I had to work ten times harder to ensure I was involved in other things. I felt a lot of power in my busyness, and when I lost it, I found it hard to fill up my days with things outside of work."

This lack of structure isn't limited to just an athlete's day-to-day routine, however: there is structure an athlete can take for granted as well across all aspects of life. For example, at the highest levels, oftentimes athletes exist in environments where their meals are portioned, prepared, and provided for them in a manner in which the athlete does not have to consider what foods they are consuming or their health benefits—someone else is handling that for them. It's simply one less decision the athlete has to make and can ensure the athlete will be competing at their highest physical levels.

However, I've heard horror stories from athletes who say when they left sports, they truly had no idea how to cook or provide relatively healthy meals for themselves: they had been in environments in which food was always provided so long and at young formative ages they were never required to learn to cook or even consider what foods they were consuming—that is, until after their playing days were over.

Similarly, a relatively unheralded and under discussed aspect of this loss of structure comes in the form of locker room experiences and even handling adult friendships. As particularly is the case with professional athletes, oftentimes its overlooked that the vast majority of an athlete's life is spent with his or her teammates. You eat together, train together, practice together, play together, go to team dinners and team meetings—your day-to-day is packed with team events during which you are surrounded with your teammates, your peers, and your friends. However, when you do retire, there is a noticeable shift in social interactions. You no longer see your friends every minute of every day, an aspect of transitional experiences in life that parallels the issues that often plague new retirees leaving the workforce for the first time.

***

When I posed a question around the difficulty of retirement to Brian Ching, former Major League Soccer MVP, United States Men's National Soccer team and 2006 World Cup starter whom we'll meet and discuss more later, he expounded on that point.

> *"What you don't realize [as an athlete] is that's it's really a lifestyle? And you live this lifestyle for pretty much your entire life. And then one day, that disappears. The moment you retire, you're not a part of that locker room and you're not going there every day hanging out with your teammates and your friends—that, that it really*

affects you because you know what's normal to you is no longer normal and you have to adjust to that."

"I think that's the biggest thing that no one tells you and points out. No one ever pointed out to me that that's, you know, it changes—it changes just in that instant. You know, it's kind of like having a kid, you know, the moment [your] kid is born, your life changes instantly. In that, as soon as you're done with that locker room, that lifestyle of going in, hanging out with your friends every day, traveling the country with your teammates, your friends, and going out and exercising and playing the sport you love is done. [Immediately after retirement] I would always tell people 'I feel like I don't have any friends anymore.'"

"Because what your friendships look like before [while playing] is completely different than what they are when you're done playing soccer, right? You don't get to see a guy every single day. You don't get to hang out with him at the coffee shop or on road trips going to dinner, you know, pretty much daily, and the adjustment is hard and it takes some time to adjust to really feel okay. You almost have to find out what a normal friendship is. You go from seeing your friends every minute of every day to seeing your friends maybe once or twice a week, if you're lucky. Mentally, that's just a really hard transition for a vast majority of [athletes]. The instant that you're off that team, it becomes a challenge of trying to adjust to a new reality and moving on from the only structure that you've known for your entire life. It is just extremely difficult on the psyche on a lot of levels."

As Ching described, this lack of structure often causes former athletes to feel like they have no direction or guardrails for handling the next phase of their life and can cause athletes to fall into depressive lulls and feelings of hopelessness.

So the big question here is how do you handle this? How do you learn to cope with a life devoid of inherent structure when your entire life has been developed in a system that demands structure, rigidness, and discipline? How should you handle this turning point and ease some of the challenges that will almost assuredly arise during your transition?

The answer is simpler in name than in practice, but you need to recreate the structure that has been removed from your day-to-day life. You need to find ways to channel the learnings and lessons from that same structure that marked the majority of your athletic life and build them into new activities in your day-to-day.

How many times as an athlete did you ever go into a game or a match unprepared with no game plan for success or even efforts to prepare for success? I'd venture almost never. In any competitive events above perhaps tee-ball, you, an athlete, practice before games. You work on improving your skills within the confines of an environment that is built for trial and error, and as you move up in levels of competition, the time and effort demanded to prepare only increases. You begin to watch film of potential opponents, practice varying skills, activities, or plays that would provide you competitive advantages in different situations. You outline plans that will lead you to success.

Handling your transition should be approached in the same way. You should treat your transition like you would treat the preparation for game day. Identify your strengths, weaknesses, areas of opportunity and growth, and develop a game plan that will allow you to utilize information in advance of a successful outcome.

***

Now how can you do that exactly? Remember our friend Marina Paul, former Georgetown University women's soccer standout and captain, from earlier in Chapter five? Marina found the biggest struggles for her transition were driven by the loss of the minutiae of the day-to-day routine that accompanied her soccer career. To put it bluntly, she missed the stuff that sucked!

"It was hard in ways that I least expected it. Like the things that I hated most, I ended up missing the most. For me [to help mitigate the challenges], I just started tapping into the things that I both loved and hated about my old schedule when I was an athlete. I literally started to rebuild that schedule for myself in a way that forced me out of my lulls."

Marina even took things a step further by creating her own playbook for success in life after sports, giving herself a way to tap into the structure that defined her as an athlete and utilizing it to build a new structure to define herself after.

> *"I think the biggest thing that I learned was that you don't have to forgo everything that you learn when you play sports or even your whole sports lifestyle. You really just*

have to figure out how to reorient your structure and your mindset to fit what you're doing now. For me, that meant creating a daily structure in my notebook, developing an almost playbook for myself where I plan out the things that I need out of each day, physically, mentally, emotionally, socially, and spiritually. I made it my mission that I needed to fulfill every component every day to be able to feel like I would be okay."

"I like to try to break it down like that for myself to give me the support and structure that I need. And it varies! For example, physical on one day could just be, like, stretching. I hate to stretch, so for me, I'll do that for my physical component for the day, or it could be getting a tough workout in on another day, but there has to be something physical on that day to check that box. But what I found was that it wasn't just the structure that helped but that it was mentally stimulating, feeling like I was designing a game plan for myself to grow, and really all of these things—the physical, mental, emotional, social, spiritual structure—creating a pseudo-playbook for myself was really helpful."

Using the same structure you learned and leaned on during your days as an athlete in your personal life after athletics and as you begin your transition, like Marina has, can provide a road map to identifying potential "landmines" that may come up while you're in it. In Marina's case, identifying all the components of herself she considered vital to her happiness and coming up with a playbook and a game plan to ensure she was satisfying each of them was the right support system she needed to get over the hump in her transition.

***

But treating your transition like you'd treat a game day isn't confined to simply your personal life: it also can be used to find success in the classroom and at work. Take Kodi Whitfield, for example, our Stanford wide receiver and defensive back turned Adidas product engineer. Kodi has found that finding ways to mimic aspects of his football routine have supported his success in his new career, from leaning on skills developed during his days as an athlete through understanding how to create a plan to ensure success in activity.

> "I'd say the biggest indication of what I've learned [from sports] came from when I got that internship [with Adidas during his master's at the University of Oregon]. Just being able to go in there, have the confidence to say, 'This is what I want to be. These are the goals that I have set for myself,' and then knowing how to work to get them or at least uncover how to work to get them. I think that's the biggest thing you learn in sports. For example, every [former player] knows that when they're in a position battle and they really want to be the top dog, that they have to work hard, spend that extra time in the weight room, in the training room, staying focused on your assignments, watching film, and really just going all in. It's kind of the same thing [outside of the playing field], you need to just keep that mentality."

> "I design shoes for a living now. So for me, in this new role, it was kind of its own position battle, gunning for a starting job. I wasn't the best artist or the best illustrator or the best product engineer, for that matter, because maybe I

didn't go to the industrial design school that others went to or have some of those learned skills that they did. But man, I saw that and just decided, 'You know what, I'm gonna grind. I'm gonna grind and I'm going to get to at least proficient, if not dominant.' And it's that mentality, that no one's going to be able to stop me and that hunger and having that will to win that you learn from sports. It's knowing what you want, and more importantly how to get where you need to be to get what you want—it's huge."

***

Hearing Ashlie, Brian, Marina, and Kodi detail similar sentiments about dealing with the difficulties of the transition experience was reassuring for me and for others as we talked through what our respective experiences were like—peer to peer, athlete to athlete.

The loss of structure and the seemingly snowballed issues that come from it were tough for me, and as evidenced in the conversations and research put into this book, tough for most athletes. But a common theme I've also recognized is when former athletes have identified their lack of structure is an issue, be it socially, personally, physically, or professionally, they typically find they are able to overcome it by creating a game plan to resolve the issue and approaching their issues in the same way they always did on the field or on the court. They've sat down, broken down the metaphorical film on what's going wrong, and come up with a strategy to overcome it. They figured out what they could do to improve their chances and how to leverage their skills to succeed... sound familiar?

CHAPTER 9

GET BORED

At this point we've discussed quite a bit about how you can approach a transition to make it more successful, how you can mitigate some of the issues that almost inevitably come with the transition, and even how you can reframe how you view your transition in general. We spent the first part of the book focused on educating about why this topic of post-athletic transition is important, what it entails, and even some heavier academic content some of you probably resent me for—I'm sorry (but I'm really not). But in my opinion, there's a component to all of those pieces of advice I don't think we've necessarily tackled head on yet. Inherently, each piece of advice we've learned from the stories of various athletes on how you can more successfully navigate your transition has touched on a component we've yet to address explicitly. That component is self-reflection.

Determining where you are in your transition experience and what happens before your transition experience is perhaps as important as any theme we've already discussed. Knowing where you are will tell you how far you have to go. Self-reflection and a truly introspective review of yourself can be the key to navigating likely one of the most difficult times of your life. By knowing where you stand, you can evaluate your shortcomings truthfully and even prepare to handle some of the roadblocks you're sure to face. Inevitably there will be things you can't overcome in preparation, but like any game you've ever played—things don't always go right; sometimes shit hits the fan and you have to improvise, that's what athletes do. But by taking stock of where you're at, you can give yourself a fighting chance to handle the speed bumps in four-wheel drive.

Hearkening back to earlier in the book, in one of our more academic chapters, we discussed the three personas of retired athletes Cavallerio et. al developed in their studies of retired gymnasts—the Entangled Narrative, the Going Forward narrative, and the Making Sense narrative. Each of these somewhat representative of the Goldilocks scenarios that can occur when an athlete goes through their transition experience: the Entangled Narrative, in which an athlete struggles to separate themselves from their athletic identity, the Going Forward Narrative, in which the athlete can comfortably move forward with their new identity, with the understanding they are more than their athletic identity, and the Making Sense narrative, in which the athlete finds themself torn between the previous two.[36]

In practice, I think there is value in taking stock of where you sit in these three buckets either before or at the onset of

---

36 Francesca Cavallerio et al., "Adjusting to retirement from sport: narratives of former competitive rhythmic gymnasts," *Qualitative Research in Sport, Exercise and Health*, 1-13, 2017.

your transitioning experience. In my interviews, I asked my interviewees, some who consider me friends, others nearly complete strangers, a rather personal question: "If knowing what you know now, you could go back and talk to yourself six months prior to your retirement and provide a piece of advice that would help that version of you through the transition, what would it be?" The responses varied pretty significantly from a tactical perspective, but mostly agreed, either overtly or inherently, it would involve some form of introspective self-evaluation to drive more successful actions.

***

For those of you who wouldn't categorize yourself as a soccer (or football, or futbol, depending on the country of origin of my reader) fan, you may not know who Brian Ching is, but if you are a soccer, football, or futbol fan, you'd know Brian is one of the greatest US-grown MLS players in the history of the league.

Born and raised in Hawaii, Ching spent four years playing his college days in Spokane, Washington, at Gonzaga University prior to being drafted by the Los Angeles Galaxy with the sixteenth overall pick of the 2001 MLS SuperDraft. Bounced between the Galaxy and the Seattle Sounders in his first three years in the league, Ching found a career launchpad and eventually a home with the San Jose Earthquakes in 2003. He became a local legend and MLS superstar when the franchise moved to Houston and rebranded as the Houston Dynamo.

In Houston, Ching cemented himself as an elite talent in the MLS and in the US soccer scene. In what he described as the "high point of my athletic career," in 2006 Ching managed to make the US men's national team World Cup roster, score the winning goal in the MLS Championship, and be named MLS Cup MVP in one calendar year. Ching was both the first Hawaiian to be drafted in the MLS and the first Hawaiian to play for the US men's national team. Ching retired in 2013 as a six-time MLS all-star with eight years and forty caps (games played) for the US men's national team, and he is considered the preeminent face of the Houston Dynamo franchise. Upon retirement, Brian immediately stepped into a role as the general manager of Houston's brand-new National Women's Soccer League (NWSL) team, the Houston Dash.

All of this is to say, Brian Ching is a big deal in the US soccer world.

However, when I asked Brian what he would change upon looking back at his unique retirement and segue into athletics front office, he offered an interesting perspective:

> "I wish I took six months and just kind of took a break and focused on just trying to get bored to really see what my passions were, instead of just kind of jumping into something initially that I thought that's what I wanted to do. But when you don't really know everything about it, it can be a tough adjustment. I was never really exposed to [my new role] on a day-in and day-out basis. So I didn't really understand what it all was, and while I thought that it was what I wanted to do, it really was just kind of a thought that I had while I was still playing. And I struggled with that experience [running the Houston Dash]. While it was great that I did have a job lined up, I don't

feel like I was given a lot of guidance. I was just kind of given a title, and it was a 'go figure it out' kind of thing."

Brian's phrasing, "Get bored," resonated with me quite a bit as I reflected back on our conversation because I think it's such an interesting way to consider the time leading up to and after the transitioning experience. "Get bored" is such a unique view on how to adjust to the transitional experience, but also a very natural one when you reconsider what it means beyond the shock value of the phrasing. Ching is suggesting by simply giving himself ample time to do nothing, to operate on a blank canvas, he would have given himself time, space, and an opportunity to discover a bit more about himself. By "getting bored," Ching and others would have the ability to do some self-discovery and really evaluate where they were in their transitioning experience and what they needed to do and where they needed to go to move forward.

While Ching's advice to his younger self was to "get bored" to identify what he would have needed to do to move forward and find his next passions in a more timely manner, others found success by being acutely aware of where they stood and where they wanted to go during their transition.

***

Max Browne, the former USC and Pitt quarterback, credits his personality and his playing days for helping him identify where he was in the process. He even attacked his path forward with a tenacity that paralleled his playing habits. Max still faced difficulties in his transition, namely in having to recalibrate his goals and his expectations post-retirement, saying,

> "It was difficult for me because you're coming to grips with the reality that a dream didn't work out. But I look at it as I failed. I didn't get it done with where my expectations were going into college football. Where I ended up, at the end of the day, I just didn't get it done, and coming to grips with that and coming to grips with the fact that my childhood dream and what I was supposed to do, whoever I was supposed to be, and whatever that means—coming to grips with that [failure] is tough and that wears on you mentally. And so, I think that is what made it difficult. And then when I decided to hang the cleats up and I had to choose a different career path, I just looked at that as kind of pivot in my life's plan."

But even with those difficulties and changing directions in his life's goals, Max has been able to channel his football experiences and turn those lessons into fuel and direction for attacking the next phase of his life.

> "It's always funny because if you asked the outside world [whether or not my transition was smooth], I think most people would say, 'Oh, he definitely had a smooth transition. Max has a lot going for him,' and all that stuff, but if anything I guess it was only smooth because of the fact that I decided not to be sitting on my ass for months at a time, wondering what was going on," Max revealed. "But, to be clear, that was a conscious decision that I made. I said to myself, 'Hey, I'm not going to be that guy.' [I decided] I'm going to go out there and move across the

country and take a minimum-wage job and be willing to sleep on a mattress in my parents' kitchen and stuff like that. I was just going to make things happen. So it was smooth in the fact that I had no lapses in time."

***

"Oh, shit, I'm sleeping in the same bed that I grew up in. I'm living at home with my parents. I have no plan. I have just ideas."

Today, Ramona Shelburne is one of the most recognizable journalists in professional sports media. A senior writer and lead NBA insider for ESPN, she is on television almost daily across ESPN's expanse of channels and programs. But as the quote above might suggest, prior to her successful venture into the world of sports journalism, Ramona was a former collegiate athlete looking for direction in her life after sports like anyone else.

Born and raised in Los Angeles, Ramona was a standout athlete and sports junkie throughout her youth, excelling in both soccer and softball in her local leagues and travel teams, and an avid sports fan, a diehard Dodgers lover. But it was in high school that her affinity and talent for softball really separated her, as she chose to pursue softball with a more targeted focus toward playing in college. Always a strong student (she was a National Merit Finalist, the valedictorian, and the student body president of her high school), as well as a supremely talented softball player, Ramona landed at Stanford University in Palo Alto, California, at the time not necessarily known for its softball team's prowess.

"When I chose Stanford, it wasn't because I thought we were going to go to the World Series. I just thought we were going to be average, like .500 (winning percentage). But you're not going there to play softball, you're going there because it's Stanford, and I was really going to be focused on the academics, setting myself up for success after softball."

But as it turns out, Ramona's experience at Stanford wouldn't be spent with softball on the back burner, as she and her teammates sparked a cultural turnaround for the Cardinal that saw the team advance to the NCAA playoffs for the first time in program history in her very first season on campus and the College Softball World Series in her senior season. Her expectations and her collegiate softball experience had shifted.

"Once we got a taste of that winning and realized we could get to the NCAA tournament and we could get to the World Series, the whole experience changed. We were all locked in. We were all in on [Stanford softball]. It became our whole life."

The success for the team was a seismic shift in approach, and soon Ramona and her teammates had built a culture of winning that came with more time and effort committed to the sport. But Ramona remained busy off the field as well, working for the Stanford student newspaper and even interning for Sports Illustrated after her junior year, with sports journalism in the back of her mind.

However, with the program's added dedication to softball only compounding her love of the sport and the success of the team, by the final weeks of her senior season Ramona knew she was in for a difficult breakup with the sport she loved, so she tried to cope with it as best she knew how—by writing.

"I kept a weekly diary every week [during my final season] and then [Stanford Athletics] had me write it and publish it for the site. In a lot of ways, it was sort of therapeutic for me, because I knew all my teammates would read it, and especially now that I'm a writer and looking back, I know that it was good for me to get those thoughts and emotions out there."

In hindsight, it's clear Ramona's future would be in writing, but when her Stanford career had finally ended, she felt aimless.

"That first year out was an awkward year for me: I was afraid to commit to a path, and I felt like I never had that college experience that others had had to kind of figure things out. I came out of college, and really what I needed was a gap year: I needed a year to not be on a schedule twenty-four-seven and not be on call. I needed some time to figure myself out."

And that's exactly what Ramona did. By her own admission, she spent a year or so bouncing around, trying new things, workouts, acting classes—"You name it, I tried it." Eventually, she landed back at the Los Angeles Daily News, working as a local high school reporter, working tough hours and difficult assignments traversing across the greater Los Angeles area, before eventually moving to "the worldwide leader in sports" at ESPN where her career took off as a longform writer and ESPN stalwart.

***

We've talked a lot about how Kodi Whitfield figured out how to bounce back and succeed in his transition from standout Stanford football player to Adidas product engineer, but there is one part of his story we haven't yet discussed. We've already discussed that upon graduation from Stanford, Kodi decided to attend the University of Oregon to acquire a master's degree; however, what we haven't discussed is Kodi dealt with a bit of adversity familiar to most athletes—injury.

Upon arrival in Eugene, Oregon, where the university is located, Kodi decided to join the local flag football team—why not, right? Kodi figured, with fairly substantiated reason, it'd be a fun way to stay involved with football and also boost his confidence a bit, knowing a former football standout at a school like Stanford would be able to dominate the local recreational league. As luck would have it, Kodi managed to tear his Achilles tendon while playing, requiring significant surgery and physical therapy and rendering him unable to walk. Why is this important, you may ask? Because as Kodi views it now, it was almost (to be very clear, extra emphasis on almost!) a blessing in disguise, because it gave him time to evaluate himself and look a bit more introspectively about himself and the applicability of the skills he learned as an athlete. Said Kodi of the experience, "I basically was, *finally*, finally an adult and had just started to realize how to use everything that I've known and really understand how the next phase of life would be for me [when I tore my Achilles tendon]. So going into PT (Physical Therapy) obviously I still have that athlete's mentality."

> "In my head I was just thinking, 'I gotta compete, I gotta get back.' But I had to realize that [at the time] it was like, what am I getting back to? I'm not going to be playing football at a high level. I'm not going to be lifting weights or running hella fast anymore. It was like 'I gotta get back to... I don't know, man?' which was really kind of tough. Piling on with that injury too was that being in grad school was truly the first time I felt as if I was able to focus on school [given football's time constraints at Stanford]. So here I was in grad school, and then I have this injury, and it took me back into that mentality of just feeling very spread thin. I feel like I'm juggling priorities again, both with rehab and physical therapy and then with school again."

But as we all know now, this story has a happy ending, as Kodi was able to lean on the skills he built as an athlete to get through the struggling period.

> "I was able to persevere and make it through to the shining point that was coming out of rehab. It felt like the grind that I was used to, and it felt like, 'I can get through this,' because I had that that college football experience. Because everything football taught me about perseverance and putting your nose to the pavement, and just grinding it out—it turned out that it was so important. Fast-forward a bit and I get an internship on the same day I graduate from school, and the same exact day, I'm cleared to walk. It just couldn't have been written any better. It gave me the chance to learn a lot about myself."

Kodi found himself in a state where he needed to reevaluate where he was to progress. He found himself stressed and in a challenging position that would require some soul-searching to move forward. And above all, he persevered and succeeded by leaning on the pillars of success he developed as an athlete—the ability to work hard, grind, and compete.

***

So what is the moral of this story? Said simply—figure out where you are in your transition story. The length and purpose of that introspective period can vary—Brian, Ramona, Max, and Kodi each took different paths and periods of time during theirs or at least wished they had—but the common thread woven in each of their experiences and lessons learned is there is an undoubtedly important experience in which you must know where you are to recenter where you'd like to go.

CHAPTER 10

THE ATHLETE'S DISTINCTION

"Athletes are great losers."

In all of my interviews, in all of my research, in every article, book, or magazine I read, I think that quote, "Athletes are great losers," is my favorite quote. It's almost paradoxical. It's contrarian, even, to everything we think of when we think of athletes. Athletes win and athletes compete. Athletes don't accept losing—except they do.

All athletes lose. They lose a lot, actually.

They lose in games. They lose in practice. They lose in reps. They lose in workouts, wind sprints, and suicides. Athletes lose a lot. But what I love about this quote, "Athletes are great losers," isn't that it seems to fight against what society thinks of when we think of athletes, as winners, champions, and heroes, but rather what is left unsaid and what the implication of the statement is.

Athletes are great losers because athletes refuse to stay losers. They refuse to stay down on the mat, they refuse to strike out and not get back in the batter's box, they refuse to get dunked on and not block the next shot—athletes always bounce back. Athletes are differentiated by their experiences, their losses, their struggles, and their comebacks. Athletes know how to lose, yes, but it is because they know how to lose they also know what it takes to win. That is what separates an athlete, and is why it is important and vital to remember even when in difficult times, like a transition experience, to lean on your strengths as an athlete and realize you have the skills to get through any of the challenges you'll face.

***

Nok Nora Duany Bassey is a colleague of mine and a former standout collegiate and professional basketball player. Nok Nora (also known as Nok), grew up in a basketball family, as one of five children, all of whom who would go on to play Division 1 collegiate basketball at well-known and prestigious basketball programs like Georgetown University, University of Wisconsin, Indiana University, Eastern Illinois University, and Syracuse University. Nok and her talented siblings were raised in Bloomington, Indiana, not far from Indiana University, where famed college basketball coach Bobby Knight had built the Hoosiers into a perennial powerhouse, and the five of them spent their days on local basketball courts, constantly playing against one another and developing an affinity and talent for the game. As she grew older, Nok dominated the local and state basketball competition in Indiana and accepted a scholarship to Georgetown University.

In DC, Nok continued to excel, seeing time off the bench as a freshman, but earning the respect of her coaches and teammates as a grinder and someone wise beyond her years. She garnered so much respect, in fact, she was voted team captain by her teammates as a sophomore, despite having not yet started a game on the Hilltop. Nok's development as a player continued, and despite being sporadically sidetracked by injuries, her impact on the Hoyas could not be overstated. Her leadership and basketball prowess separated her on the court and in the locker room during her time at Georgetown—so much so Nok was able to earn an offer of a professional contract playing overseas for a professional team in Portugal.

She spent a year playing with the team, in what amounted to a sports culture shock to Nok, as for the first time in her basketball career, due to the playing schedule of her Portuguese league, she found herself with more free time to explore new passions, such as traveling Europe and sightseeing with her fellow teammates. At the advent of the next season, however, Nok decided to leave the sport due to the wear and tear that was placed on her body and the toll the different style of play and facilities presented on her past injuries. At this time, Nok had made the decision to redirect her talents elsewhere.

"I was scared," she said. "I was scared of figuring out what was next and trying to figure out who I was outside of basketball."

But a larger conversation with her family marked a turning point for Nok, as they challenged her to look deeper at the person she had become during her athletic career.

"You are more than a basketball player," they explained to her. "You are bigger than just what you've done on the court."

It was this topic in the discussion with Nok that spurred her supplying my favorite quote of the journey that was writing this book. "Athletes are great losers," she said. This quote came amid a larger conversation, and really the concept I want to ensure all of you reading understand, especially those who are going through the transition now or will soon be going through one, is you have to remember the things you've learned as an athlete separate you and have taught you invaluable lessons you'll be able to lean on in even the most difficult times.

***

Athletes build a mental toughness and confidence that is rarely replicated, and often challenged, but never falters. Take Chris Conte, the former NFL defensive back of the Chicago Bears and Tampa Bay Buccaneers, whose story we told earlier in the book. Conte had a widely successful NFL career by any standard, playing eight years in a league with an average career span of less than three, and starting for a vast majority of his career.

Chris was by any and all standards a standout football player.

However, two plays in Chris' career created an unfavorable public perception of his abilities and caused undue damage to his reputation. The first of these plays came in a game against the Green Bay Packers, an archrival in a game with playoff implications. A teammate was out of position on a key play in the game, and Chris, attempting to cover for his teammate's mistake, was the nearest defender in a play that altered the outcome of the game. The play was out of his control, but he was viciously scapegoated by the media and the "fans" who targeted him with hateful notes and attacked his character and abilities online.

The other play in which Chris was dealt an unfair hand was a game in which he was playing on a severely injured leg. Chris tried to play through injury because his team desperately needed him out there and had no alternatives should he have been unable to play. Chris caught a bad break and without the luxury of a stable knee to stand on, was thrown out of position by an opposing player within direct camera shot of the nationally broadcast game and was vilified by the announcing booth, the media, and "fans" again.

The outcomes were decidedly poor, but both were not his fault, by and large out of his control, and yet he was responsible for bearing the weight of both burdens on his shoulders. Chris had every reason to be angry and resentful in both scenarios—but how did Conte respond? By ignoring the garbage opinions of those who didn't matter, by being a true professional and taking accountability for things that weren't even remotely his fault, by being tough enough to deal with problems others wouldn't be.

He understood the only critiques and opinions that mattered were the ones of his teammates, his coaches, and his own—all of whom were aware of the circumstances of the failure. Chris handled failure, embarrassment, and loss like only an athlete can—by brushing it off, learning from it, and bouncing back.

***

Sound familiar? Max Browne dealt with similar criticism and disparaging commentary from national and local media during his short opportunity as the starting quarterback at USC. But Browne took the same route Conte did and let the experience toughen him, and he now uses it in his professional life: "My experiences in sports have definitely tied to professional success. Putting it in perspective now, I mean, when you get benched on national television, when you're the biggest bust in college football history, the idea of getting yelled at by your boss is like a joke. It's all in perspective, and for some people, getting yelled at by their boss is the worst thing that will happen all month. And to me, I can just shrug it off, and that's the beauty of that perspective. And it's that perspective, that sports has given me, that football's given me."

Funnily enough, Browne wasn't the only athlete I spoke to who made that same point, as former Boston College rower Anthony Perasso had a similar life lesson imparted upon him by his sporting experiences, saying, "I think the biggest thing I learned is the lesson of detaching negative feedback from yourself. I've heard enough bad things come out of coaches' mouths to learn not to take negative feedback from my boss personally. In fact, that negative feedback just means they care and want you to improve. If they stop giving you any sort of feedback, then you're really a lost cause."

***

The other component that makes athletes particularly unique is their willingness to grind and pursue excellence relentlessly. Browne pointed that out specifically in his own experiences, saying, "The work ethic [is vital]. I mean, it's fun being a football player, sure, but with both football and school it really is a lot of work. Those 6 a.m. workouts and all that, it just gives you a different mental wiring. That same wiring is what drives that pursuit [of excellence], really wanting to be the best in your industry, wanting to be the best in your position. That mentality—it's a different work and skill set, I guess you could say, but I've made a conscious effort to try to transfer that mentality over to my new industry, and I told myself then, every day, every morning of college athletics, I would wake up trying to be the best quarterback I could possibly be. Now I wake up trying to be the best person and worker I can possibly be."

Mary Ricks, the UCLA softball star turned president of a six hundred million dollar real estate company, expounded on how exactly that mindset translates into her business and recruiting for her firm now: "One of the things now, as a senior member of the team, in real estate, when we look to recruit people, I'm always pushing for and love to recruit athletes, because you just know that competitive athletes are dedicated. They know how to work hard and play for a winning team. We've been talking about the team—it is all about the team. And it's usually [athletes], they're not complainers—they're tough. There's an inherent toughness to them, and I think in business you just have to have all of these things. And so, to me, in any business, an athlete really has a little bit of an edge, especially on other students coming out of out of college, because they've been there, they've done all that hard work that business eventually takes. Getting up early takes being dedicated, takes making sacrifices. Working late, or having to work on holidays, which I've done and my colleagues have done many, many times. It's just part of the deal, whatever it takes for the team. Now my team is Kennedy Wilson, so whatever it takes to make Kennedy Wilson successful, I am willing to do. I am willing to do whatever it takes. Anyone that I know that has been a former athlete has that, and I think generally those people have been really successful for the most part because of it."

As Mary explained, athletes are great "grinders"—people willing to put in the work and do uncommon things to get uncommon results. Athletes understand team dynamics amounting to the equivalent of masters in the subject; anyone who has spent as much time in locker rooms mixed with teammates from wildly diverse backgrounds has developed the ability to understand what it takes to set aside personal goals and opinions to ensure the team's victory. Athletes know the value of hard work.

Hayden Pascal, a former crew captain from Georgetown University, may have said it best when he explained, "Success is a byproduct of your effort, not a measure."

Max Browne echoed this statement when he challenged the adage hard work pays off, instead reframing hard work provides a peace of mind. This is a lesson learned from the trials and tribulations of a life lived in the sporting world, particularly in sports as team-centric as crew or football, but known by all athletes. There will be times in which you make all of the right efforts, all of the right moves, and still lose—that has happened to every athlete who has played their sport for as long as elite athletes have. But what separates an athlete is their ability to lose, even when it's out of their hands, and bounce back, learning from their failures and turning them into successes.

If there's one lesson to be taken from this book, it's that you as an athlete have developed skills that make you uniquely suited to handle transition experiences and adversity—not just leaving athletics behind, but other experiences as well—as well as or better than others. You can handle this particular transition, leaving your sport behind, by relying on tenets you learned during your playing days: lean on your people (Trust your team); figure out what makes you tick (Know your own strengths); find your team (Embrace the locker room); treat your transition like game day (Prepare like you want to play); and know where you are (Watch your own film).

As an athlete, you are conditioned to deal with challenging situations, uncertainty, artificial hurdles, and unforeseen obstacles, and to reach the highest levels of sport, you have undoubtedly conquered some of them and lost to others. But as an athlete, you also are a great loser. You do not fear failure: you embrace it and understand failure is simply an opportunity to improve. These words are my own, but they stand on the shoulders of the stories of other athletes who have been told throughout this book.

As a now or soon-to-be former athlete, the most important thing you can do to move on from your days as an athlete is to remember the qualities, characteristics, and endeavors that made you one in the first place.

CHAPTER 11

ATHLETES' THOUGHTS, UNFILTERED

—

As this book comes to a close, I'd be remiss not to address the role of those who offered their time, thoughts, and wisdom to me and to profess my gratitude throughout my book-writing process. I had the great fortune to lean on the words and stories of athletes far superior to me in every way, shape, and form. It is with that in mind I'd like to offer this final chapter as a repository of profound thoughts and wisdom that some of my willing interviewees were willing to impart upon you, the reader, as a gift from their brains and their experiences to you. So below and beyond you'll find a collection of advice, tidbits, and guidance from a select number of the former athletes I had the distinct privilege of speaking with.

Even if you managed to make it through the previous eleven or so chapters and thought no piece of the written word I have provided was worth a single grain of thought, I implore you to at least embrace this section as a saving grace opportunity for the book, as I once more ask my interviewees to allow me to stand on their shoulders and shout their stories to the masses. So without further ado, I present to you Athletes' Thoughts, Unfiltered.

AARON BARNETT
Sport: Baseball
Team: Pepperdine University
Current Occupation: Bullpen Catcher, New York Yankees

Notable Quotes:

> "My time as a player has had a huge impact [on my post-playing career.] I've learned some other lessons from my playing days: work hard, be open-minded to new information, and to respect your teammates. Baseball is undergoing a massive transformation right now, with data analysis and interpretation playing a huge role in developing players. The work ethic I learned from sports, as well as the willingness to accept new ideas, has helped me internalize this information."

> "I challenge [you] to make sure [you're] parting ways with [your] sport for the right reasons. If you have no love for it and no desire to keep playing, fine. But if your reasons are anything like mine (e.g., the wrong reasons)—'I need to get started on a stable career right now,' 'I'm scared of a few years passing in which I still haven't made it in my sport and I could've spent that time starting a career,' 'I did well academically, therefore the right thing to do is to start a career outside of athletics,'—I would caution against being so quick to leave your sport. One thing I

learned in my brief time in business, and even in my roles since then, is that life moves slower than I'd thought as a college kid. There's ample time to pursue a passion and see how far you can take it, and if it doesn't work out, there's ample time to find a non-athletic lane to be successful, too."

ANGELA YANG

Sport: Track and Field, Cross Country
Team: University of Rochester
Current Occupation: Strategy Consultant, Accenture

Notable Quotes:

"Teamwork, competitiveness, and coachability are the three key traits I picked up from sports that have helped me in my professional career. The most important thing I learned was that you need to be a team player to be successful—in terms of both winning and creating a happy team. I learned how to work with different people, how to play to the strengths of individuals and the team, how to mitigate the weaknesses of the team, and how to adapt quickly as an individual and team. Reflecting on the past few years, I would not be where I am today if I had not followed my coaches. Similar to how one would do pre-season training or build a base in running, it lays the foundation for the next step in your career. I am always appreciative of the parallels between my sports and professional career and it has definitely helped me navigate my career thus far."

ANTHONY PERASSO
Sport: Rowing and Crew
Team: Boston College
Current Occupation: Social and Editorial Strategist at Peloton Interactive

Notable Quotes:

> "So much of work is interpersonal skills and handling negative feedback and just shutting up and getting the work done, operating on a team where you're used to being a part something greater than the sum of its parts. You're gonna have a leg up on people who aren't used to that type of environment. I think going forward at work I'm comfortable mentoring interns or younger employees because we had that sort of dynamic on our rowing team Also, understanding that yeah, the next two months might suck, but it's gonna be great when it's over and you'll be rewarded then. That's rowing, that's work."

ASHLIE WILLIAMS
Sport: Volleyball
Team: Georgetown University
Current Occupation: Integrated Marketing at Live Nation Entertainment

Notable Quotes:

> "I think it's important for me to note that volleyball is a predominately white sport. And as a Black athlete in that space, when I think back to what it felt like to step on

the court, I am reminded that it was the one place that gave me back exactly what I gave in. Those nine hundred square feet represented the only space where no one could make me feel like I didn't belong. I worked my ass off, and it was always clear when I made a contribution to the team. Don't get me wrong, I experienced my fair share of racist coaches, coded comments, and biased treatment. But not having to be looked at as different, even if it was only for twenty-five points at a time, was important to my education on how to successfully navigate the world. Credit being given where credit is due is not always as clear cut in the real world as it is on the volleyball court. However, whenever times like that arise, I take that same tenacity from the court and confidence in my worth to create ways to ensure my hard work is not lost in the grand scheme of things."

BRIAN CHING
Sport: Soccer
Team: US Men's National Soccer Team, Houston Dynamo (MLS), Los Angeles Galaxy (MLS), Seattle Sounders (MLS), Montreal Impact (MLS), Gonzaga University
Current Occupation: Entrepreneur, Financial Manager

Notable Quotes:

"Get Bored."

"Don't be afraid to seek help—it's normal to struggle."

CAMERON WALKER:
Sport: Football
Team: University of California at Berkeley
Current Occupation: Operations and Strategy Consultant at K1 Investment Management

Notable Quotes:

> "You're more than just an athlete. There's more to your journey than just what you did on the field."

CASEY KUHNS
Sport: Football
Team: Georgetown University
Current Occupation: Technology Account Manager, Oracle

Notable Quotes:

> "The most formative point of my athletic career would probably have to be learning what it takes to be a D1 athlete. The discipline and drive you learn never goes away, and it has stuck with me even in retirement. I also was not the best D1 football player, but I was able to contribute to the team because of my work ethic. I try and bring that same mentality to anything I do."

> "I think the realization that I was going to have to motivate myself to work twice as hard just to keep up with the much more talented players at Georgetown was the best thing that ever happened to me. I wouldn't have had the same work ethic today if that didn't happen. Sales is a

profession that constantly asks you to motivate yourself, so I think my success in sales is directly correlated to what I went through at Georgetown."

CHRIS CONTE
Sport: Football
Team: Chicago Bears (NFL), Tampa Bay Buccaneers (NFL), University of California at Berkeley (CAL)
Current Occupation: Finishing Degree at University of California at Berkeley

Notable Quotes:

"My advice would be if you have a dream you want to go for, go all in and make it your all day, every day."

"I think the best way that I've found dealing with that is trying to get involved in other sports. It's still finding that competitiveness. And so, like, I've stayed working out and I try and train like I'm still an athlete. I'm still trying to compete at that high level, maybe not the same exact way, but in a way that, you know, is difficult and that I'm challenging myself."

GABRIELA ELVINA
Sport: Softball
Team: Georgetown University
Current Occupation: Program Associate, Softball Operations at Washington Nationals Youth Baseball Academy

Notable Quotes:

> "Focus on every aspect of being a student-athlete. Student first. Athlete second. But also, go have some fun, kid. It's okay to go out and meet some new friends. Don't say no to an opportunity to do so. This is your time. Don't waste it."

HAYDEN PASCAL
Sport: Rowing and Crew
Team: Georgetown University
Current Occupation: Senior Financial Analyst CBRE

Notable Quotes:

> "You will never know when you are at rock bottom at the time, but your response to it will come to define who you are. Confidence is a muscle that grows when you exercise it in the face of adversity. It cannot be faked, though people will try. You don't even have to succeed in your task to build it—it's not about the outcome, it's about how you handle adversity and how you grow from the process. Success is a byproduct of your effort, not a measure."

> "Sports also don't have to be out of your life. Pick up another sport, try different things."

KODI WHITFIELD
Sport: Football
Team: Stanford University
Current Occupation: Footwear Designer, Adidas

Notable Quotes:

> "You're an expert at building relationships from playing sports because you will encounter people from so many different walks of life brought together in one arena. The fact that I can find a way to relate to, for example, a kid from Louisiana who looks nothing like me, who grew up completely different, and we could still find a way to relate as teammates and work towards something common—that's huge. You're just incredibly personable and now you have the ability to attract people around you who will be invested in your success as well."

> "Stay in the deep end. Focus on the task at hand, rather than the outcome. Remember that there are so many steps before the podium. Remember all those lessons you have learned in football, learn in sports, and just trust in it, trusting yourself and it all work out the way it's supposed to be."

MARINA PAUL
Sport: Soccer
Team: Georgetown University
Current Occupation: Consultant, Accenture Federal Services

Notable Quotes:

> "I also think time just helps. Which sucks, especially when you're in it, but it really does help, and finding that

community that will allow you to be that same person is probably the most important thing."

"It's gonna be hard in ways that you least expect it. Like the things that you hated most, you're gonna end up missing the most. This whole process, it's honestly really about learning how to fall in love with yourself again, because until you do that, you and it's an everyday thing, and it's going to be a forever thing, but until you do that or start on that journey, it'll be hard."

MARISSA HEWITT
Sport: Lacrosse
Team: Brown University
Current Occupation: Regional Director, Harlem Lacrosse; Founding Board Member, Pacific Edge Lacrosse Association

Notable Quotes:

"The most important lessons that sports taught me was that sports teach you to do things that aren't for yourself. You sacrifice and make personal decisions for the betterment of others and the betterment of the whole."

"I really do think the hardest thing to find is what's going to fill that competitive void, you know, that juice—so chase things that make you feel that way."

"Understand you're going to experience discomfort—mental and physical discomfort [when you retire]. When those routines and structures and that level of fitness and *competition are no longer readily available, knowing that that's what's happening gives people a lot of hope, and answers a lot of questions. It's normal to deal with that discomfort!"*

MARY RICKS
Sport: Softball
Team: University of California, Los Angeles (UCLA)
Current Occupation: President, Kennedy Wilson Holdings

Notable Quotes:

> "I would tell somebody to try to get into some other league of some kind, whether it's, like, join a tennis club or playing a softball league or, you know, a pick-up basketball league—do something where you can continue playing sports competitively, so you can have that sports and athletic outlet while you're starting to work, because I think it's really hard to go from just full-on your life has been sports ever since you were a little kid, to working full-time."

MAX BROWNE
Sport: Football
Team: University of Southern California (USC), University of Pittsburgh
Current Occupation: Broadcaster and Radio Host, Pac-12 Network, Sirius XM Radio

Notable Quotes:

"They say, oh, like if you don't have a plan B, it means you're planning for success. And we hear that from the one guy that makes it, but for that one guy that makes it, there's so many other guys that bought into that same quote that now their life's in a shitty place. I'm not a fan of that; I think you can have multiple plans—they're not mutually exclusive. You can still shake someone's hand, when you're in it in as a college athlete, you can still go to class, you can still do that stuff. And you can still be the hardest worker on the football team. They're not mutually exclusive."

"Go find the human being that you're like, hey, I'd love to live his life here and twenty years, ten years, fifteen years. Go work for that person, try to get in their ecosystem, try to get in there in their network and do whatever it takes to get in there. I think life has windows of opportunity and that opportunity, right when you start playing sports, before you get kids and wife and all that, or spouse—that's an invaluable opportunity to go make some moves and test some things."

MICHAEL CHABALA
Sport: Soccer
Team: Houston Dynamo (MLS), Portland Timbers (MLS), DC United (MLS), University of Washington
Current Occupation: Founder of Sphere

Notable Quotes:

"Know your self-worth."

> "Understand the pursuit of where you want to go, and treat the pursuit of success off the field the same way you do on the field."

> "Surround yourself with the right people."

MYRIAM GLEZ
Sport: Swimming
Team: French/Australian Olympic Team
Current Occupation: Founder, Chairwoman of Athletes' Soul

Notable Quotes:

> "Those who will transition [out of sports] the best are the ones that are the most prepared."

> "The soft skills you've learned as an athlete are more valuable than you know. You can always learn to be an accountant or master really technical work, but those soft skills are a major asset that you've developed since a very young age."

NOK NORA DUANY BASSEY
Sport: Basketball
Team: Georgetown University, Liga Feminina de Basquetebol (LFB, Portugal)
Current Occupation: Consultant, Accenture Federal Services

Notable Quotes:

"Athletes are great losers."

"Know that you are more than your sport."

RAMONA SHELBURNE
Sport: Softball
Team: Stanford University
Current Occupation: ESPN, Senior Writer, NBA Insider

Notable Quotes:

"A lot of stuff that you learn as an athlete stays with you your whole life. Your athletic career might be over, but your life as an athlete, the things you learned, your ability to be scrappy, your ability to handle adversity, and the ability to just compete will always stay with you."

ROB SGARLATA
Sport: Football
Team: Georgetown University
Current Occupation: Head Coach, Georgetown University Varsity Football

Notable Quotes:

"Be fearless, don't be afraid to walk up to anybody and say hello—you are different as an athlete, don't shy from it."

> *"Lean on other athletes for advice; don't be afraid to leverage your team's connections."*

TYRELL WILLIAMS
Sport: Football
Team: Georgetown University

Notable Quotes:

> *"You've always been more than just an athlete—you are successful as a human because of who you were as an athlete."*

ACKNOWLEDGMENTS

When I set out to first write this book, I had a hard time believing I'd ever actually reach this point, writing my acknowledgments, and thanking all the folks who made this possible. But here we are, and I am typing away, humbled and grateful by all of the support, love, and help I've received through this book-writing process.

First and foremost, to my family—thank you for all of your support both during this journey and over the years. I could not be more lucky to have a family who cares about me and supports me the way you all do. I love you all.

To my friends and loved ones—you all have been there for me through all of the ups and downs, the great memories, the not-so-great memories, and even the blurry ones, too. I am eternally grateful for all of you and your support, and I hope to be as supportive to all of you as you have been to me.

To Eric Koester, Brian Bies, Carol Thompson, and Linda Berardelli—thank you, thank you, thank you, thank you. For pushing me to do something I wasn't sure I could, for giving me an opportunity to challenge and surprise myself, for providing an opportunity to meet new people and hear their stories, and for turning my jumbled, clumsy thoughts into a beautiful book I can be proud of. I am forever grateful for the time, effort, and passion you put into my individual journey.

And thank you to everyone who: gave me their time for a personal interview, preordered the ebook, paperback, and multiple copies to make publishing possible, helped spread the word about Bouncing Back to gather amazing momentum, and helped me publish a book I am proud of. I am sincerely grateful for all of your help.

Aaron Barnett~
Alejandro Wiley
Anderson de Andrade
Andrew Finnegan
Andrew Green
Andrew Magaña*
Angela Yang~
Anna Peaslee
Anthony Perasso~
Ashlie Williams~
Barry Goldsmith
Bennett Gagnon
Bill Connelly*
Brett Solomon
Brian Ching~
Brian Held
Caitlin Finnegan*
Cameron Walker~
Casey Kuhns~*
Chad Bracken
Chris Conte~
Chris Villalpando
Christian De Rosa
Christina Mangels
Cody Hanson

Connor Niemann
Dan Sprotte
Dana Traversi
Daniel Finnegan*
Danny Davis
David Chung
DeMoni Falls
Doane Liu
Elliot Solandt
Emilio Moran
Eric Koester
Erin NaPier
Ethan Douville
Gabriela Elvina~
Hannah Gropper*
Harley Traven
Hayden Pascal~
Isabella Yozzi
Jack Brennan*
Jack Kuhns
Jeff Rhee*
Jimmy Gehrels
Jimmy McLaughlin
Jo Vosburgh
John Loizeaux

Jon Stott
Jordan Portner
Julie Hulse*
Karen Finnegan
Kathy Finnegan
Kelly Mandala
Kenneth Muoneke
Kodi Whitfield
Korey Bowles
Kori Hudson
Kristen Canales
Kristen Cope
Kyle Nolan
Laura Ellison
Leanne Sheward
Liz Duvall
Mara Hofman
Marie Bartz
Marina Paul
Marissa Hewitt~
Marlo Williams
Mary Ricks~
Matthew Buckman
Matthew Rollings
Matthew Stoffers*
Max Browne~
Michael Chabala~
Mike Westra
Morgan Hines
Myriam Glez~

Nok Nora Duany Bassey~
Patricia Salvaty
Peter Kropp
Phil Bernstein
Ramona Shelburne~
Regina Finnegan*
Robby Kolanz
Robert Longwell
Sachi Carlson
Scott Cleeland
Sean Wilson
Sekhar Ray
Shawn Paul
Simon Halls*
Steve Solomon
Tay Centineo
Taylor Soergel
The Klein Family*
The Lopes Family*
The Montanez Family
The Shelton Family*
Tim Finnegan*
Tommy Jesson
Travis McCormack
Tyrell Williams~
Vincent Girardi
Vincent Tzeng
Woody Liu
Yasmeen Sharara

Key: *multiple copies/campaign contributions, ~featured interviewee

APPENDIX

CHAPTER 1:

Bell, Lydia and Tom Paskus. "Results from the 2015 GOALS Study of the Student-Athlete Experience." Report presented at the NCAA Convention. (San Antonio, Texas: Grand Hyatt San Antonio, 2016).129. http://www.ncaa.org/sites/default/files/GOALS_convention_slidebank_jan2016_public.pdf.

Irick, Erin. "NCAA Sports Sponsorship and Participation Rates Report." NCAA.org. Accessed March 6, 2020. https://ncaaorg.s3.amazonaws.com/research/sportpart/2018-19RES_SportsSponsorshipParticipationRatesReport.pdf.

Vikraman, Deepak. "Kobe Bryant last game: Read the entire transcript of Kobe's farewell speech." International Business Times. Apr 14, 2016. https://www.ibtimes.co.in/kobe-bryant-last-game-read-entire-transcript-kobes-farewell-speech-674620.

CHAPTER 2:

Cambridge Dictionary. s.v. "sport (n.)" Accessed Mar.15, 2020. https://dictionary.cambridge.org/us/dictionary/english/sport.

Hattersley, Chris and Dave Hembrough, Kaseem Khan, Andrew Picken, Tom Maden-Wilkinson, and James Rumbold. "Managing the transition into retirement from sport for elite athletes." (Sheffield, UK: Sheffield Hallam University, 2019.)

Accessed May 21, 2020. https://www.researchgate.net/publication/333967975_Managing_the_transition_into_retirement_from_sport_for_elite_athletes.

Oregon, Evelyn Monteal. "An Examination of Athletic Identity and Identity Foreclosure Among Male Collegiate Student-Athletes." (Chapel Hill, NC: University of North Carolina at Chapel Hill, 2010). https://doi.org/10.17615/xadh-8a5.

Quinn, Sam. "Michael Jordan vs. LaBradford Smith: A look at the Bulls legend's revenge against an imaginary opponent." CBS Sports. May 17, 2020. https://www.cbssports.com/nba/news/michael-jordan-vs-labradford-smith-a-look-at-the-bulls-legends-revenge-against-an-imaginary-opponent/.

CHAPTER 3:

Cavallerio, Francesca and Ross Wadey and Christopher Wagstaff. "Adjusting to retirement from sport: narratives of former competitive rhythmic gymnasts." Qualitative Research in Sport, Exercise and Health. 1-13. 2017. Accessed May 4, 2020. DOI: 10.1080/2159676X.2017.1335651.

Chadiha, Jeffri. "Life after NFL a challenge for many." ESPN.com. May 31, 2012. Accessed May 2020. https://www.espn.com/nfl/story/_/id/7983790/life-nfl-struggle-many-former-players.

Ermler, Kathy L. & Carolyn E. Thomas., "Institutional Obligations in the Athletic Retirement Process." Quest, 40:2, 137-150. 1988. DOI: 10.1080/00336297.1988.10483895.

Gallup Inc., "A STUDY OF NCAA STUDENT-ATHLETES: Undergraduate Experiences and Post-College Outcomes." 2020. Accessed May 2020. https://ncaaorg.s3.amazonaws.com/research/other/2020/2020RES_GallupNCAAOutcomes.pdf.

Imperfect: The Roy Halladay Story. Directed by Mike Farrell and Brian Rivera. Aired May 29, 2020, on ESPN.

Stambulova, Natalia B. and Tatiana V. Ryba and Kristoffer Henriksen, "Career development and transitions of athletes: the International Society of Sport Psychology Position Stand Revisited." International Journal of Sport and Exercise Psychology. March 2020. DOI: 10.1080/1612197X.2020.1737836.

Schwarz, Norbert. "Feelings as information: Informational and motivational functions of affective states." in Handbook of Motivation and Cognition edited by E.T. Higgins, R Sorrentino, Guilford Press, 1990. Accessed May 13, 2020. https://www.researchgate.net/publication/232591956_Feelings_as_information_Informational_and_motivational_functions_of_affective_states.

Vickers, Emma, "LIFE AFTER SPORT: DEPRESSION IN THE RETIRED ATHLETE." Believe Perform (Blog), Oct. 14 2013. Accessed June 2020. https://believeperform.com/life-after-sport-depression-in-retired-athletes.

Webb, William M., Suzanne A. Nasco, Sarah Riley, and Brian Headrick. "Athlete Identity and Reactions to Retirement from Sports." Journal of Sport Behavior 21, no. 3 (09, 1998): 338-362. Sept. 1998. https://search-proquest-com.databases.library.georgetown.edu/docview/215873304?accountid=142883.

CHAPTER: 4

Chadiha, Jeffri, "Life after NFL a challenge for many." ESPN.com, May 31, 2012. Accessed May 2020. https://www.espn.com/nfl/story/_/id/7983790/life-nfl-struggle-many-former-players.

Schlossberg, Nancy K. and Eilnor B. Waters and Jane Goodman. Counseling Adults in Transition Linking Practice With Theory. New York: Springer, 1995.

CHAPTER 5:

Amick, Sam, "Kobe Bryant finds 'Muse' beyond basketball artistry." USA Today. Feb. 25, 2015. Accessed June 2020. https://www.usatoday.com/story/sports/nba/lakers/2015/02/25/kobe-bryant-los-angeles-showtime-documentary-cinema-director/24002331/.

Associated Press. "Kobe Bryant bouncing film ideas off Spielberg, Abrams, Bruckheimer." ESPN.Com. May 20, 2016. Accessed June 2020. https://www.espn.com/nba/story/_/id/15626468/kobe-bryant-bounces-film-ideas-gets-advice-steven-spielberg-jj-abrams-jerry-bruckheimer.

Manfred, Tony, "Kobe Bryant Cold Calls Business People To Ask Them Questions About How To Be Successful." Business Insider. Jul. 22, 2014. Accessed May 2020. https://www.businessinsider.com/kobe-bryant-cold-calls-people-2014-7.

CHAPTER 6:

Chabala, Micahel. "Our Story." Sphere.Club. Accessed May 6, 2020. https://www.sphere.club/our-story.

CHAPTER 9:

Cavallerio, Francesca and Ross Wadey and Christopher Wagstaff. "Adjusting to retirement from sport: narratives of former competitive rhythmic gymnasts." Qualitative Research in Sport, Exercise and Health. 1-13. 2017. Accessed May 4, 2020. DOI: 10.1080/2159676X.2017.1335651.

www.ingramcontent.com/pod-product-compliance
Lightning Source LLC
LaVergne TN
LVHW011836060526
838200LV00053B/4054